PAST RELATIONSHIP PRESENT YOU

Starting Afresh with Fruits from the Old Tree

JOY CANFIELD, PH.D.

MANUFACTURED IN THE UNITED STATES OF AMERICA

First *Image Cascade Publishing* first edition published 2018.

Library of Congress Cataloging in Publication Data

Canfield, Joy Elaine, 1961–

Past relationship - Present you: Starting afresh with fruits from the old tree

(Self Help)

ISBN-10 1-59511-888-8

ISBN-13 978-1-59511-888-2

TABLE OF CONTENTS

Introduction	7
Why Do You Look Back?	11
Closure	
Are You Acting Like You?	18
Questioning and Learning Exercises	22
Love	40
Breaking Things Down	48
Did You Self Care?	56
Equals? Fairness? Power Balance?	70
Mutual Respect and Trust	87
Response to Externals:	
When Family or Friends Disrespect	
Consistency	107
Intimacy	118
Satisfaction → Communication → Happiness?	135
Stonewalling	
Looking Ahead and Charging Forward	148
References	163

To my clients

Throughout your relationships,

you have an infinite capacity to love and learn.

Introduction

I remember sitting in the veterinarian's office awaiting an appointment, a pup on my lap; a kitty in a carrier. Standing before the reception desk was the "parent" of a small tan and white long-haired guinea pig. She was gingerly cradling the soft and silent creature in a light blanket so that only the furry head was exposed. The blanket was fielding her tears as she conveyed to the staff that her Georgie was still not well and the veterinarian seemed to have given up hope. She implored that she had done everything she possibly could for the tiny patient... she rarely slept... ensuring that her pet received his medicine and vitamins around the clock. They must be wrong?

Her words conveyed that she thought she had done it all. Yet there was a tone that seemed to say that maybe she hadn't done enough. Maybe she could do more. Maybe she could have tried harder. Maybe it was her fault. And her wistful hope reiterated, somehow he had to be ok.

Every living entity in that waiting room felt her sadness. Every living thing absorbed the despair and pain afloat. The people. The awaiting cat and dog patients. The office cat. Even the plants seemed suspect of soaking in this woman's transparently communicated pain. No one spoke other than the receptionist who murmured some empathy filled words. My eyes met with the wide eyes of each of my daughters. I shifted my glance from one to the other. We shared a sentiment it seemed as the woman trailed off, "He's only 5 and a half. He could live longer – I know he can. I can't give up." The other people in the waiting area looked at their feet or into their magazines; a few directly toward the guinea pig. There was emotion in the air; there was a sentiment in their postures; there seemed a word on their minds – it was "inevitable."

Interestingly, my family had recently been talking about the life span of guinea pigs. Friends and neighbors had spoken of their beloved pets with some swapped stories circulating of parents replacing the guinea pig with a look alike to shield their children. My own children had worried over this moral dilemma wondering what is loving and kind to do. Yet their discussions among themselves and their friends had yielded some consistent data: That it was very likely that the warm and fuzzy family member would not outlive them – nor was he likely to outlive the family schnauzer. It was so sad, said they, yet in their pure and worldly wisdom of ages 10 and 11, they noted the inevitability.

Relationships that are healthy have the propensity to live on. Relationships that are less healthy, may need some intervention, meds, or vitamins. Relationships that are unhealthy, may have an inevitability of a conclusion. The latter may be difficult to distinguish, and the discerning process is not exact.

Here we will examine your views on your past relationship. Here we will awkwardly stand with an earnest ear and a gentle eye of empathy. We will try not to look into our magazines nor down to our feet. We will look clearly at you and find clarity in your history. And the "we" will really be "you" looking into the mirror.

You have spent some time asking yourself and others many of the questions that we will examine. Yet we will try to take these thoughts and questions and answers and non-answers and see how you may cultivate them; we will see how you may move forward. And we will aim to help you move forward with the discoveries and riches, leaving behind the limitations and impurities.

Your relationship is behind you. You are free. There were benefits from the relationship, there were costs, and there were many things in between. Here we will examine your former relationship from the standpoint of cultivating your growth, development, and learning. Rest assured, we are not trying to paint your memories with a happy brushstroke. We will aim to view the relationship with a theme of what you have gained and what you may bring forward.

What is a relationship anyway? First, we could say that a relationship is not completely tangible. A relationship is the result of two entities being mixed together in some "relating" way, for a period of time. Definitions of "relationship" tend to begin with, "The way in which..." or "A state of being in which..." There is little to concretely grasp in the definition of relationship. Yet it seems accurate to say that relationships have great influence on human beings.

If a relationship concludes and you feel pain, it may be tempting to wipe away the timespan of the relationship. Yet in doing so, you would be wiping away many positive and worthy discoveries. Some of those discoveries may be the key to your next door.

Our approach here will be one of contemplating your past relationship from the view on the other side – a healthy informed side. We will examine:

- The identifiers predicting a relationship's conclusion or good health
- Alternative thoughts, emotions, and behaviors regarding these identifiers
- The discoveries and acquisitions that are derived from relationship experiences
- How these discoveries may help you in the present and future.

This process may be helpful if you are struggling with the reconciliation of:

- What happened?
- Why? And why me?

- What did I do wrong? Or right?
- Whose fault was it?
- What could I have changed?
- What should the other person have changed?

Closure

Many people have difficulty moving forward when relationships end. Some report having lack of closure regarding the relationship and the reasons for its dissolution. Others feel remorse believing that time was wasted and the love rendered was undeserved.

Examining the predictors, the conflicts, and the management of conflict may help you understand more about closure as well as how to draw learning from the experience. Yet the *unanswered or unanswerable questions* may actually be *the answer* to why people have difficulty gaining closure. That is, the relationship's theme of ambiguity may be why people struggle with the ambiguity of the relationship's ending. Philosophers in phenomenology and existentialism see ambiguity as an integral part of the human condition (Heidegger, 1927.) Yet it may be frustrating in a relationship *not* to know whether key elements exist within it.

Persistent ambiguity in relationships may lead to a fear induced preemptive strike when one or the other person lacks tolerance for the unknown (Halevy, 2017.) This is particularly true when one partner desires to know if he or she is secure in the relationship. We could empathize with the person who fears the worst in the relationship and ultimately sabotages self or other. Perhaps such a person can no longer bear the fears and just wants the unknown to end. We might counsel that person to talk about fear, yet the response may be that he or she is too afraid to know. What a conundrum.

When you think about how the mind works, you may recognize how swiftly people like to know things. Sometimes they prematurely attach meaning to a very small part of the greater picture. They are so desperate to decide what has happened that they disregard or discredit some of the other parts of the picture. Ultimately, they label a small element as the reason for the whole thing. As we sort through relationship puzzles, we will refrain from overly emphasizing any one part. Rather, we will explore each part of the puzzle as evenly as we may and occasionally stand back to gain a broader view.

As you are coming to this juncture already knowing that your relationship has ended, we will abstain from trying to jolly you into thinking that everything is going to be all right. We will more accurately emphasize that many parts of your life remain healthy and hope filled.

To Be or Not?

If you have ever sat with a person who has received a terminal diagnosis, you may have known the impulse to say, “Everything’s going to be all right.” Then you may have stopped yourself short and revised your statement to, “Everything is going to be...” You might have quickly pondered Hamlet’s “to be or not to be” statement. Perhaps you considered that “not being” is still “being.” To that terminal patient, you may have extended comfort, reminding that "to not be" is still being something, somewhere, yet in a different form.

While your relationship is not to be, we may remind you that *you* are here and are to "be" – perhaps in a different form. Thankfully, that is in the here and now and your presence is abundantly tangible.

But why are we examining all of this? Why bother if it is over?

That reason may be unique to you and your future. It may be unique to your future healthy relationships. Yet most experiences yield dividends. They offer insights; they cultivate knowledge. It may not be accurate to say that you must experience something difficult so that you may understand life. Yet traveling down a rocky path helps you to understand and better recognize smoother terrain.

Finding purpose and meaning in your life is an evolving lifelong process. Finding meaning in difficult circumstances is part of that process. Remember that your process is unique and *we* are here to champion your uniqueness; to help you find your way to your unique happiness. *For you, there is not just one way – there are infinite paths to your happiness. And your unique happiness increases the likelihood of finding your unique future.*

Are You Acting Like You?

When your actions match your basic core principles, theorists refer to this as congruity (Gawronski & Strack, 2012.) This feeling of synchronization gives you the feeling that you are acting like you. This congruity influences your maximizing your potential. With congruity, you can be your most authentic you. When you have congruity, you self observe your actions, you recognize yourself, and others recognize you by your familiar behavior.

When people deviate from their core principles, there is a strange feeling of cognitive dissonance that results. Cognitive dissonance is that uncomfortable feeling that something is not right. It feels akin to having a jagged piece of glass caught in your sleeve. The urge is to quickly remove it. One option for resolving cognitive dissonance is to restore congruity between actions and core principles. For example, if you are hearing your words and tone yielding negativity and disrespect, you quickly correct your words and tone by matching them with your positive principle of respect. You might revisit a conversation by saying, "I can't believe I said that about him. I apologize for my name calling and being so abrupt. I realize that I took out my frustrations of the day on him. I was out of line."

An alternative method of relieving cognitive dissonance is to rationalize or justify the incongruity. Rather than changing your words and tone, you might say, "Well, he's a jerk and he was rude to me first. He deserves it! Besides, I'm tired of guys like him!" If rationalization and justification of cognitive dissonance is done repeatedly, over time, you could inadvertently readjust and normalize your behavior to the "new way of doing things."

When people recognize that they are out of synch with their fundamental core principles, they have the opportunity to make changes and re-synchronize themselves to their basic beliefs. Steps to restoring congruity to our foundational principles begin with *awareness*. Once we are aware that our actions lack congruity to what we fundamentally believe, we may then consider alternative methods of communicating who we fundamentally are. Once we consider the behavioral alternatives that reflect our beliefs, we may gradually recondition our automatic responses to triggers that activate our thoughts and behavior. Over time, we may normalize a response that is accurate, more positive, and congruent with our positive core principles.

As you consider your past relationship and explore the patterns and habits within it, think about this concept of congruity – examine when you sounded like yourself versus when you did not. These discoveries will be helpful to you as you evolve and develop in your personal and interpersonal existence. As we examine the principles that predict positive relationships in the next chapters, we will continually examine the matter of congruity, cognitive dissonance, and methods to resynchronize your actions with your positive foundational self.

Questioning and Learning Exercises

Let's explore some of your questions regarding your past relationship and its ending. If your relationship was a tree, we could see the results of this process as the fruits that have been derived even if the tree is now firewood. Your questions likely lack absolute answers, yet we may examine them more accurately on a sliding spectrum. As there are few absolutes, shifting from side to side on a fluid continuum gives you more freedom to adjust your perceptions and influence your future. Try not to worry over what you write or how it sounds – just do a little free writing exercise and see what happens.

Writing has been recognized throughout psychology and the medical community as a viable release of traumatic stress effects (Van der Kolk, 2014.) Take note of this benefit and its relevance to your moving forward journey. Calm and rational writing exercises may help you organize and regulate your emotions as well as improve your overall physical and cognitive well being. By slowing down and calmly assessing your history, your brain can actually work more efficiently (Goleman, 1995.) Your high alert emotional drivers (your amygdala of the temporal lobes) let go of your executive functioning skills (prefrontal cortex,) and your capacities to organize and plan out your thoughts are enhanced. By breathing and focusing calmly on your writing, impulsivity is reduced, and your emotional reasoning is improved.

What happened?

The *what* may not be easy to pinpoint or define. Nonetheless, let's focus on facts and accurate phenomena. While the corresponding emotions and pain are less tangible and measurable, the facts will keep you honest. Think about what happened. Write about it now.

Why..... Why me?

Why did this happen? Write out your thoughts regarding why you believe the relationship ended.

As you consider "why me?" focus on accuracy and facts. While you may feel that you are a casualty in the relationship's ending, the reality is that you are fully intact and combing through the facts so that your future is better informed. Chances are that your partner did not target you as the recipient of his or her negative actions. You each were likely caught up in the ripple effects of evolving life events. By considering yourself as whole and unabridged, you will help prevent a premise of viewing yourself as an altered or victimized person. It is empowering to know that you are enriching yourself from the experience rather than piecing together a set of damaged parts. Write about how you felt about yourself immediately after the relationship ended. Then write about how you feel about yourself now.

What did I do wrong? Or right?

As you consider the discoveries from your relationship, aim to focus on the fluid continuum. Remember that dichotomy (all or none) is rare. When possible, adjust your terminology from right or wrong thinking to "different." "I was right; he was wrong," becomes, "He had a different view," or "She had a different method." Write out your thoughts about what you would do differently in your relationship. Write about what you would do the same.

Whose fault was it?

Focusing on negative things and blaming is easy to do. Considering your relationship as a fluid continuum will help you shift from one end to another. When you hear yourself saying, "It was ALL her fault," try shifting to, "She had different ways of doing things and I didn't agree with them." And, "He did things that really bothered me. I just do things so differently than he did." If you believe that you or your partner was at fault, write about what your feelings are. Aim to use the terminology of "different" and "disagreed."

What could I have changed? Was it *me* who changed?

When reflecting on your relationship, start with yourself first. Think of yourself as one who has core foundational principles. Your primary responsibility is in retaining congruity with your basic core self. To retain congruity, you aim to consistently enact your core beliefs. If you believe in respect, you demonstrate respectful behavior. If you believe in fairness, your thoughts and actions are fair. If you believe in honesty, your words are honest and your tone matches your principle of respect.

If somewhere along the way you changed *the method in which you enact* your positive principles, then we would say that you have evolved over your developmental lifespan. As a child, you handed your favorite turtle to your grandpa to show love. Now as an adult, you may speak of love or help him with household chores. Your method has changed, yet the core principle is constant. Yet if you *deviate from your core principles*, you would benefit from examining why this deviation occurred. If you believe in trust yet your behavior defies trustworthiness, then you will also benefit from exploring how to resolve this incongruity. Going forward in any future relationships, you will feel more comfortable and authentic if you are synchronized between who you are and how you demonstrate yourself.

If you think that you changed during your relationship, write down some thoughts about this. Write about what you would change within yourself during the relationship.

Did your partner change? What needed to be changed? If you believe that your partner changed, write about this. If you believe that your partner needed to change, write down your thoughts about this. Write as factually as you can.

Re-read your thoughts from time to time. As a human, you have and will continue to develop throughout your life span. Conflict and adversity have the potential to inspire growth. Most likely as you search for honest and accurate answers to your relationship questions, you will find derivatives that will puzzle you as well as strengthen you. It is difficult to prevent feelings of regret, yet cultivation of negative events creates a yield of insight. Each time you write and read and re-read your reflections, envision yourself as the competent farmer preparing your crops to be healthy for a robust harvest. You may not be able to influence external elements, but you may indeed influence the preparation process.

Vignette:

Maryanne's thoughts drifted back to the past years – why had she done the things the way she did? If she had kept up a better front, maybe she would not have blown it.

Sid: What did you do all day?

Maryanne: Oh, just the usual.

Sid: Like what?

Maryanne: What what?

Sid: Like why is the pile of laundry still thrown in the middle of the sofa?

Maryanne: …… ohhhh yeah…. I've totally been meaning to get to that.

Sid: (*Silence. Then drifting into the kitchen.*) Do we have some chips?

Maryanne: Uhhhh, or yeah, I think we…. Or no, I meant to get some. I'll definitely do that tomorrow.

Sid: Did Irma come today?

Maryanne: Yeah, she was here this afternoon.

Sid: Did she pick up the dry cleaning?

Maryanne: Oh no! I completely forgot to remind her. I'll see if she can stop by tomorrow before she goes to the MacKenzie's.

Sid: Okay. (*Vacantly gazing through the window.*) Mar?

Maryanne: Yeah?

Sid: This weekend maybe we could talk about making a couple of changes.

Maryanne: Okay. I mean, what do you mean?

Sid: I guess it's been a long time since we reassessed things here.

Maryanne: You mean you and me "we?" You mean like around the budget or something?

Sid: No, I mean, since the kids graduated from high school, we haven't really talked about making changes here.

Maryanne: I still don't know what you mean.

Sid: Okay. Never mind. We'll just talk later. It's fine. I think I'm just tired.......

Maryanne now looked back on what this non-eventful dialogue might have been. The kids had been away to college and almost graduated around that time. Sid had been working his way up in his company becoming more stressed and quiet and losing his more upbeat demeanor seemingly along with his hair. Was that a breaking point? Had Maryanne missed it? Was she to blame? Was it all her fault?

Like many couples, when Sid and Maryanne had married, each were working. As Sid began thriving in his career, their first child, then the second came along. Maryanne transitioned from working full time to part time and ultimately it seemed less cost effective to work and more efficient to be a stay at home mother. It was agreed upon from both sides. Then came a move deeper into the suburbs, soccer games, home room mother jobs, selling candy for fundraising, looking into colleges, visiting colleges, a few family road trips, then off went the kids. Sid continued to work and Maryanne continued to field the weekly housekeeper, the handyman, the roof repairs, and the garden cleanout. It was functional to some degree but never took flight into a new chapter of coupledom. Ironically, the "weekend talk" never happened and Sid kept trudging out in the morning, returning quietly in the evening. Occasional holiday visits from the kids distracted everyone yet nothing was discussed regarding the relationship. Until two years ago.

As Maryanne told it, Sid had an affair. Not a fancy affair, just an affair. A drab one that mimicked Sid's demeanor. But it was an affair and for Maryanne, that meant the end. So Sid hired his attorney suggested that Maryanne hire her own and within a year or so, there was a divorce.

Those are the facts, and over the subsequent months, Maryanne's emotions have run the gamut. Sid lives in a small apartment closer to his office and Maryanne has a smaller house near the old family home. Her bank accounts are healthy enough and the house is paid in full, yet Maryanne was wondering now if it was her fault. If only she had vacuumed and dusted more often. If only she had cut back on pastries. If only she had baked *more* pastries. If only she had kept working. If only she had kept jogging. If only she had done the laundry better. If only she had been younger or prettier. If only.

While there are no quick answers, there is little gained in blaming and thinking in absolutes. No doubt somewhere along the way, Sid and Maryanne adjusted their self views – as do most people. The view in the mirror certainly does change over time. A changed self view can indeed be projected onto someone or something else – "It is *her* fault that I've lost my edge....." "It's *his* fault that I can't find my motivation...." "My wife doesn't do anything for me anymore, but Judith sure thinks I'm cool...." "My husband is such a jerk, but my students totally respect me."

When our self view changes, it does not necessarily mean that we have lost ourselves. It may be that we have limited or disallowed our evolution and growth. We may be limiting ourselves by blaming others and not taking personal responsibility for adjusting to changes in circumstances, age, appearance, or the relationships around us.

What would you tell Maryanne? What would you say to Sid? What are the discoveries for each of them? What limitations may they leave behind?

Interestingly, Sid returned to Maryanne's doorstep asking for a second chance. After resisting the temptation to slam the door in his face, Maryanne asked him into her small bungalow and sat him down for tea.

Maryanne told Sid that, no, she didn't want to get back together, yet surprisingly her thoughts were less about his infidelity and more about her own decision making process. She said that at first she blamed Sid for everything that had gone wrong in her life and in their relationship. Then she found herself scrutinizing her own behavior and blaming herself. By now, she was not exactly blaming herself, yet she had made some discoveries about how easily stuck a person may become. Sid apologized if he had caused that and while Maryanne appreciated the gesture, she took back the responsibility and said she needed to be her own coach and encourager. No question, she did not appreciate his past behavior and those actions had spoken for themselves. Yet Maryanne preferred to take hold of the obstacle and create her own self navigated path.

If there was ever a "next time" with anyone, Maryanne said that she would look that person straight in the eye and talk about the drifting off rather than cocooning in the avoidant patterns of her history. She said that on some level, she had known that Sid was bored and discouraged yet at the time she had blamed him and burrowed more deeply into her personal lackluster cave. She could nearly laugh now about the couple's mirrored avoidance, yet she still did not agree with his methods of avoidance and his ultimate deception.

She still had work to do on developing her capacity to trust yet she could only take responsibility for her own actions and zone of influence. Maryanne said that this is what she is doing and Sid could make his own decisions about his area of responsibility. Yes, in the beginning she thought that Sid had totally blown it. Then she had drifted into believing that she had totally blown it. Now she was just working through what was her own area of responsibility. Taking away the teacup and saucer, Maryanne noted that since she no longer had a housekeeper, she would need to say goodbye for now as she had chores to do before she was off to her job.

Avoidance behavior may take many forms within a relationship. It is easy to take the path of least resistance and dodge the conversation that you do not wish to have. Yet avoidance tends to deepen and perpetuate negative thoughts and emotions. What could be a simple, honest conversation may brew its way into a deeper conflict. As you reflect on your past relationship, consider any patterns of avoidance – in yourself or your partner. What could have been done to prevent such patterns? How could communication have been re-engineered? Would a regular check in have helped? As you ponder these patterns as well as other positives and negatives, stay focused on accurate thinking and areas of personal responsibility. It is easy to fall into a self blaming or other blaming mode. By thinking factually, you will be able to consider the context of circumstances, sort through the content with a proportionate eye, and accurately consider your zones of personal responsibility.

Love

What is it? Or is it an it? Some say it's the greatest thing we have – those who watch love filled films; those who devour romance literature; those who read scripture; those who live their lives. Words that are attached to love may include:

sublime

benevolence

virtue

affection

unselfish

loyalty

passion

altruism

eternal

fulfillment

honesty

greatness

pure

endearing

warmth

charity

attachment

infinity

compassion

Think about what love is to you.

Regardless of how we define it, love seems to be something living creatures are interested in having. And thankfully we have an infinite capacity to love and be loved. This infinitude is heartening as we consider the conclusion of a relationship and the discoveries we have made therein.

In the film and stage play, *The Heiress*, Catherine is enrapt with the fortune hunter and idler Morris. She rebukes her wealthy dying father's doubts of Morris's authenticity, shunning his threats to disinherit his daughter. When Morris abandons Catherine, believing she is no longer wealthy, Catherine recognizes that his "love" was false and greedy. When he returns realizing her ultimate inheritance, Catherine feigns interest and accepts his proposal. Yet when he arrives to retrieve her for marriage, he finds a dark and closed Washington Square townhome. Rather than accepting a love filled with ambiguities and falseness, Catherine seals her heart with the infamous words to her maid, "Bolt it Maria...." "Bolt the door Maria."

Catherine believed in love despite her father's cruel form of loving and protecting her. She continued to believe in love, despite her suitor's shallow method of reciprocating. Yet when he returned after abandoning who he thought was a poor woman, she viewed the circumstances accurately. She spoke the apparent painful truth: Morris was back with his same old story; his same old lies. Yet this time, now he wanted her love. That was the kicker. Bolt the door.

What does this mean? What does this tell us about love? Perhaps this is a story recognizing that love must be honest. If it is entangled in attachments to tangible things and evolving states of being, then it may lack the security and safety of consistency. Think about the consistency of love in your past relationship. Was love volatile? Was it constant? How did the demonstration of love change? Was it attached to tangible things or parts of you or your partner that would inevitably change?

In another venerable motion picture, *Now Voyager,* Bette Davis -- in a role of the once awkward now sophisticated spinster Charlotte -- gently scolds her beloved (though married) Jerry when he asks, "And will you be happy, Charlotte?" She replies with a seasoned, pragmatic form of love, "Oh Jerry, don't let's ask for the moon. We have the stars."

Charlotte believed in love despite her mother's dominating method of loving her. Her mother had attempted to suffocate her development, sequestered her, and obstructed her path toward having true love in her life. When a proper and approved suitor came along, Charlotte considered his proposal, yet she knew that it was a proposal of convenience, practicality, and superficial pleasantries. Alternatively, she could not be with the man she genuinely loved – at least not in her home and daily life. Yet she could instead have his daughter's presence and she could love him through her. She loved the young girl, identified with her vulnerability, and knew that she had Jerry's love, albeit from afar. This was her galaxy of stars; in this she was sufficiently fulfilled.

Perhaps in this story we see that love, in its most authentic form, may not have the conventional demonstration according to societal norms. While Charlotte could have traded in this authentic love for a practical, convenient relationship, she chose authenticity. Again, the theme of honesty prevails.

Years ago, I recall speaking with a neighbor regarding her love for a colleague. He was older and encapsulated in a system that seemed to deny open acknowledgment and reciprocation of a potential relationship. Yet she was happy. I asked her how she thought this could be? She said that so long as she could be around this person, she felt happiness. She acknowledged having a full life of her own and that she would continue pursuing her objectives. Yet she did not wish to break away from her love, even though it was not clearly and openly reciprocated. But said I, how about talking with this person? What about exploring a possible future? Maybe things could be different? Yet she was far ahead of me noting that bucking the system was not wise and further, she was patient and enjoyed her life as it was. If he was free and she was free in five or ten years, then it would be worth the wait. To a bystander, this seemed an unfulfilled love. Yet to that person, the love was honest and free of negativity. She took a "don't trouble trouble" approach and felt fulfilled believing in her love and hoping for a potential future. Do you think that this woman had the stars and lacked the moon? Did she fear that the moon would obstruct the stars? Do you think it is possible to have both?

Consider your thoughts on love. Think of who you love and how you love that entity – a family member, a friend, perhaps your pet. Who do you feel most comfortable loving? Who loves you just as you are? Think of how you feel when you are loved.

We sometimes recognize how deeply we love someone after that tangible life has ended. The loss accentuates the love and the pain feels proportionate to how greatly we love that person. Death may be bigger than humans, yet love manages to defy it. Love is certainly a commanding thing. Love may be intangible, immeasurable, and undefinable, yet it packs an everlasting powerful punch.

When you consider your past relationship, you may recognize that you continue to love that person. You may feel aggravated with yourself for loving that person. Or you may even say that you loathe that person. Yet the intensity of that feeling implies that there is a strong emotion remaining. It may be helpful for you to acknowledge these intense emotions. They are valid and they are real. Trying to avoid them or push them down is likely unsuccessful – examining them accurately and clearly may help you move forward.

When a relationship concludes, you have decisions to make about the love you had or still have for that person. Do you believe that it was a waste? Do you regret extending your love to him or her? While it is simple to negate the worthiness of loving your former partner, if you see love as an infinite thing, then there is no loss of your love capacity in having loved someone. And if the action of loving uses a muscle, then you have invested in that muscle and it is strengthened. No doubt the pain tells you that something went wrong with the muscle. Yet it was not love in itself that caused the pain. Something may have gone wrong within the delivering or the receiving, yet if it was love, then it had a positivity about it that may be retained. And if you have strengthened your "love muscle," then you have done something positive and healthy for yourself and for all whom you love.

Breaking Things Down

Most overwhelming obstacles are better managed by breaking them into smaller parts. Even a hefty emotion may be broken down into more manageable parts. As you think about your relationship and its positives and negatives:

- Sort through each part
- Focus on equalizing the parts
- Stand back and size up the big picture with a more focused lens.

As you consider the feelings you had or continue to have regarding your relationship, you may discover why those thoughts and emotions persist. Contemplating the broader context and sorting through its smaller bits of content may assist you in your future relationships: with romantic partners, friends, colleagues, and family.

Vignette:

Carol opened the jewelry box buried in her sock drawer. She quickly slammed it closed and smashed the drawer on her fingers. And cried. For hours.

After a pint of ice cream and a box of tissues, Carol walked back into her bedroom. She opened the drawer with her bandaged hand and reached for the now dented box. Inside she found her engagement ring and wedding band, a tiny bag of rice, a browning engagement picture, and an envelope with some crushed, powdery, and musty rose petals. In another envelope – not so old and not so crushed – she saw the handwriting of a different woman and the faint scent of a perfume Carol had never worn. It was an ironic blending of the beginning and the beginning of the end. All in a box that was now permanently sprung open.

What to do with the beautiful and what to do with the ugly? Funny that there was no sign of the middle. Where were the ticket stubs from plays and movies? Where were the doggy bags from favorite dining spots?

Where were the grocery receipts containing bargain finds at the bulk food store? And where were the running shoes of two people who trained together for the half marathon?

Carol might have some more crying to do over the beauty. She may cry or slam drawers over the ugly. Yet ultimately it may help her to break the memories down into parts.

A relationship is many things. It is filled with two people who are each many things. The greater proportion of a person is predominately positive; so too is the greater proportion of most relationships positive. It is so easy to idealize someone with whom we are smitten and equally easy to vilify the person who has disappointed us.

As you consider yourself in your past relationship, aim to focus on accuracy. As you think about your partner and different aspects of the relationship, try to be factual and realistic. It may seem pain relieving to vilify someone who is associated with pain. At times, you may find yourself idealizing parts of your relationship as well. Yet as you are making discoveries about yourself, the person, and the relationship, you will find more accurate information by being factual, honest, and fair.

Many people enter a relationship with an eye on the good and exit that relationship with blinders to the good and a microscope on the bad. Yet at this juncture, an accurate view of the beginning, middle, and end will help you sort out the positives, moderates, and negatives.

Most likely you found something good about your former partner. Early in a relationship, so many facets of the person unfurl – fresh, new, and mostly positive. As your relationship continued, those positive features likely persisted, yet something overshadowed them and tinted your lens. This may have happened in your partner's view of you as well. By considering these facts carefully, you may find a more accurate view of each person's area of responsibility. This process helps prevent self blaming or blaming others. Taking personal responsibility for yourself will help you to accurately view your thoughts and actions and proactively evolve you forward.

The below models illustrate the visual shifting of a relationship's content areas. Though specific content areas diminish in positivity, the overall context remains moderate. It is notable that some content areas remain positive and moderate although key areas become negative. As you consider your past relationship, draw your own models. Consider the overall context of each module then consider specific content areas and how they evolved over time.

SHIFTING CONTEXT AND CONTENT AREAS

The "Smiths'" Assessment

Assessing Relationship Context – Reviewing Specific Content Shifts Over a Nine Year Time Span

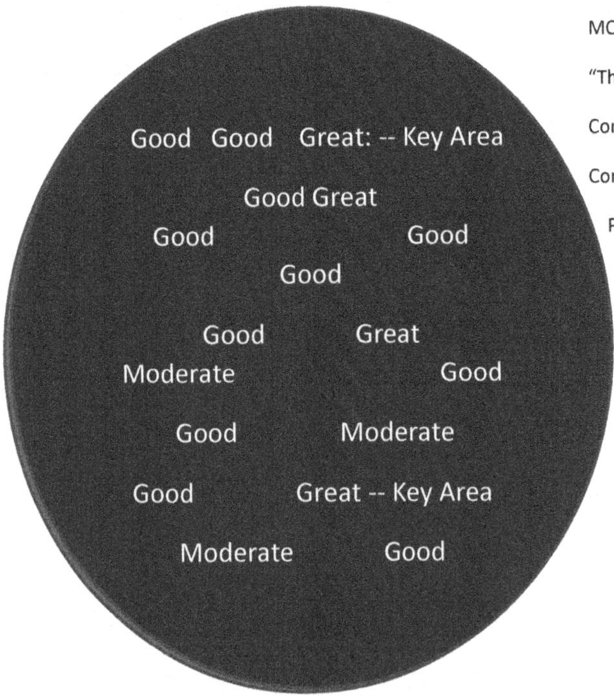

MODEL 1

"The Smiths"

Context Positive

Content Areas

Positive

MODEL 2

"The Smiths"

Context Positive

Content Areas
Mixed

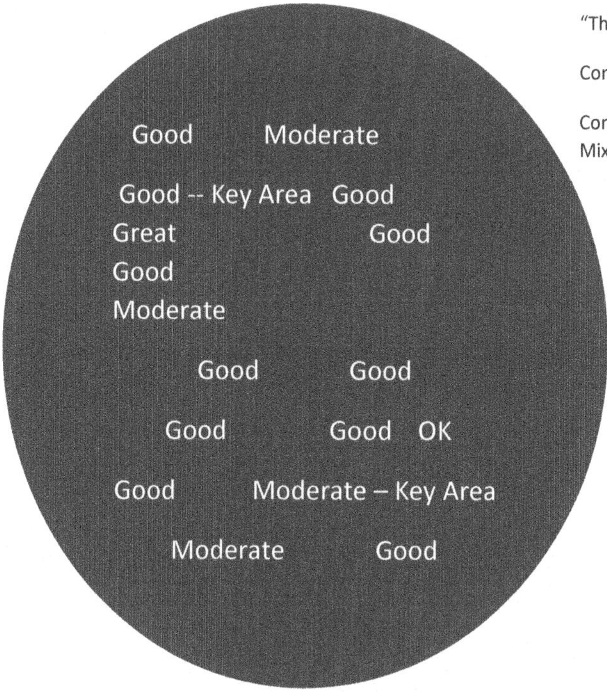

MODEL 3

"The Smiths"

Context
Moderate

Content Areas
Mixed

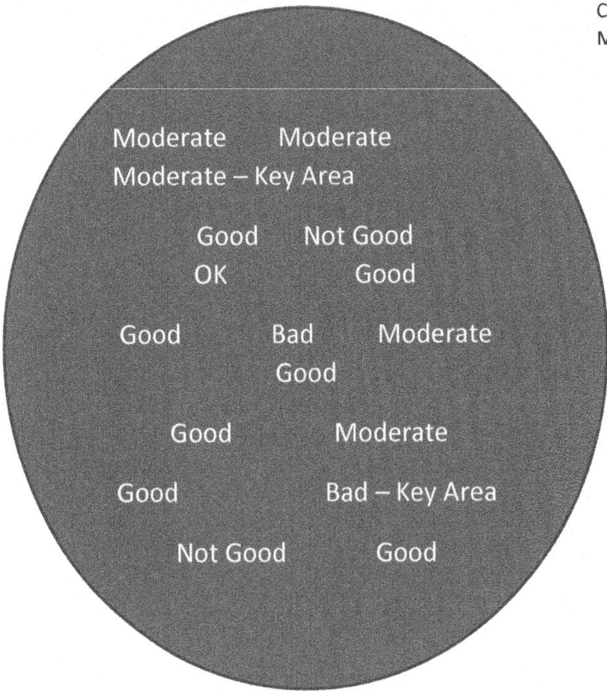

Did You Self Care?

Taking personal responsibility for self refers to the flight attendant's familiar admonition: "Oxygen mask to self first before rendering to others." In your past relationship, did you respect your responsibility to self care? While it may feel uncomfortable or self serving for you to think about taking care of yourself, it is notable that self love and self respect are necessary in order for you to love and respect others. If you are struggling with your capacity to love and respect yourself, why is this?

Self Care

Consider practices of self care in your past relationship:

- Did you take care of yourself physically?
- Did you tend to have sufficient sleep?
- Was your appetite healthy?
- Did you eat well and enjoy it?

- How was your fitness regimen? Did you have one? If so, was it the regimen you desired? If not, why did you sacrifice this aspect of your life?
- Think about your general health. Did you seek medical assistance when you needed it?
- Did u create your own appointments for medical care?
- Did you or your partner self sacrifice in order to maintain the household and/or care for the family?
- Were there conflicts in your relationship about your self care or the other person's self care?

Couples may find themselves in a long suffering deliberation examining their personal hardships. Each person may fall into a one-upmanship debate of personal struggles. Self sacrifice may become a theme and the label of martyrdom may be bandied about. Pressure to outdo the other may be an unsustainable phenomenon. And feeling that one person tends to draw the short stick may lead to resentment.

Coexisting can be difficult for any humans. Chronic conflict may spiral a couple downward toward a loss of empathy and perspective taking. When there is a perceived unevenness in who does what and who self sacrifices, each person may get hurt. One or both partners may neglect basic self care leading to a deepened cycle of pain. A relationship is neither healthy nor sustainable if a partner must compromise his or her health in order to maintain the relationship.

Vignette:

Margie: I'm heading to the gym.

Mick: Ohhhhh... well look at you.

Margie: What do you mean?

Mick: Well here I sit after working my brains out all day and off you go to your precious little gym.

Margie: Leave me alone.

Mick: No problem. Happy to do it. Bags packed and out of here when you get back. Or don't bother, how about that?

Margie: You're so messed up.

Mick: You've made me that way.

Margie: I can't stand your behavior any more. You resent every single thing I try to do to be healthy.

Mick: Do it on your own time. I come home to see my wife and off you go to hang out with who? Big buff guys? Who cares about it (stomping toward the back room, with obscenities flowing.)

Margie drops her gym bag.

What to do?

The usual.

Walking into the kitchen. And stopping. About to turn around.

What are the options?

Sigh.

> *Opening the freezer, she retrieves the pork chops; peels the plastic from the package; and plunks the lump into a dish to thaw for dinner.*

What happened here?

Devaluation on many levels. Lack of fairness. Disrespect. Distrust. Loss of perspective taking. Did Mick not believe that Margie should take care of herself? Did he understand what Margie's objectives were? How could Margie have responded to her responsibility for self care? What was Mick's actual concern within the dialogue? What could this couple have done differently?

Healthy relationships encourage mutual self care with each person assuming his or her personal responsibility. Partners encourage one another to take care of themselves, championing these efforts. Self sacrifice tends to appear in settings that encourage martyrdom. Imagine the family reunion that hands out plastic trophies to the family that struggled the most to attend the gathering. Whose car broke down? Who had to beg their neighbor to watch the cat? Who had to bargain with her boss to allow an early Friday departure? Who sweated and struggled the most? Sometimes pain and suffering are rewarded in relationships.

Self sacrifice may be an indicator that a relationship is declining. What does it mean if one person badgers the other until he or she is reduced to tears? The badgering partner then relents. He or she may even comfort the wounded. What does this mean? It could be compared to boot camp: Beat 'em down then build 'em up -- though the building up may not occur. This practice may be compounded by low self esteem, ultimately leading to resentment (Righetti & Visserman, 2017.) Do you think that this is a form of abuse?

> *While physical abuse in intimate relationships is an indisputable and unacceptable human rights violation (Campbell, 2002,) emotional abuse is a precursor to physical abuse. Emotional abuse can include verbal assault, ridicule, control, isolation, and the use of personal information for degradation (Follingstad, et al, 2005.)*

Consider your past relationship – think about patterns of demeaning or mocking followed by apologies and overcompensation. If your relationship had a pattern of berating or punishing until one person broke down, this was an unsustainable, unhealthy pattern. This is a discovery which is worth pondering as you move forward in any relationship. When a partner *embraces your growth and encourages your development*, your personal long term well being is predicted to improve. The opposite is true when your partner obstructs your capacity to develop thereby decreasing the likelihood of your growth (Feeney, et al, 2017.)

As you consider what is healthy in a relationship, *write down your thoughts and views on your personal responsibility for self care.* Write down interpersonal patterns that are unhealthy as well as healthy habits to be retained.

- Think about mutual encouragement within a respectful relationship.
- Consider potential methods to self care.

- What are methods to convey encouragement and compassion within a healthy relationship?

Relationship communication need not be boot camp. Ridiculing, mocking, and sarcasm tend to devalue a listener. While the communicator may intend to be playful or teasing, there is strong potential for the listener to hear a tone of disrespect. Think about the tone of communication in your relationship. What changes could have been made to increase mutual encouragement, respect, and empathy regarding self care and in other areas?

Alternate Mick and Maggie Vignette:

Mick: Where are you going?

Margie: The gym.

Mick: Why now? I just got home.

Margie: I just got home myself and I really want to work out.

Mick: Can you do it later?

Margie: No, I've made a commitment to myself that I'm going to exercise at least 4 times a week.

Mick: What about your commitment to me?

Margie: (*Silence.*)

Mick: What does that mean?

Margie: I want to say something but I'm afraid to say it.

Mick: How come?

Margie: Because every time I say something that you disagree with, you get mad.

Mick: *Every* time?

Margie: Okay, sometimes.

Mick: What is it?

Margie: Well I really wish you could try to understand why this is important to me.

Mick: What is?

Margie: Taking care of myself. I really want to try to take care of myself. It feels so much better to be fit.

Mick: Why do you want to be fit?

Margie: What do you mean?

Mick: I mean.... Are you wanting to look better for other guys?

Margie: WHAT?!

Mick: Well, I mean, you go down to that gym in those shorts and who's there?!

Margie: (*Silence, then,*) You mean, you think I'm wanting to get in shape so that other guys will look at me?

Mick: Maybe.

Margie: When have I ever given you that idea?

Mick: Uhhhhh..... Well, I've heard about that sort of thing happening and the girl leaves the guy.

Margie: Which girl? Which guy?

Mick: Okay. So maybe I'm a little mad.

Margie: At who?

Mick: At those guys down there. I mean... maybe I'm a little jealous of guys I don't know down at the gym.

Margie: Why would you be jealous of people you don't know?

Mick: So.... Well maybe they'd look better than I do and you'd be attracted to them.

Margie: Mick. C'mon. I have asked you dozens of times to go to the gym with me. Haven't I?

Mick: Maybe two times.

Margie: Mick!

Mick: Okay, maybe a few times.

Margie: Well, do you want to go with me?

Mick: No.

Margie: But then why are you mad?

Mick: I don't know.

Margie: Well I do. You want to go but you are afraid to go.

Mick: I'm not afraid of some stupid gym.

Margie: No.... you're afraid of yourself maybe.

Mick: (*Silence.*)

Margie: Let's go. (*Silence.*) I want you to go.

Mick: (*Silence. Then,*) Maybe I could go just this one time.

What happened *here*?

In the first vignette, Margie's desire to self care appears to be disrespected and overridden. Yet in the second scenario, Mick's fears are dominant and seemingly unrelated to Margie's commitment to fitness. In this vignette, it seems that Mick was not comfortable to state his fears. They may have been multifold: Fear of Margie's self improvement, fear of the attention that she could receive, fear of his inability to compete with such a setting, fear of being compared to others, fear of

Margie's potentially leaving him, fear that Margie did not perceive Mick in a positive light, fear of self perceptions.

Having fear is AOK. When fear is identified, the next steps are to consider the general context of fear and then sort through specific fears. This is a shared process in a mutually communicative relationship. Yet the environment must be consistent and safe to create an atmosphere for sharing such scary thoughts. Some couples find themselves conducting the pre-emptive strike under such conditions. That is, one of the partners may speak out the fear ahead of its reality. In this case, Mick might have stated, "You are having an affair with someone from the gym. I know it." These statements may be inordinately alienating to the listener whilst being falsely relieving to the speaker to speak out the worst case scenario. While the accuser may feel better to state his greatest fear, his partner is at risk of being deeply injured by such an accusation. If trust and faithfulness are paramount in one partner's foundational principles, being accused of distrust could wreak havoc in the relationship.

As you reflect on your relationship dialogues, consider the guidelines of mutual respect, trust, fairness, consideration, empathy, perspective taking, and honesty. Think about the forms of communication that encourage partners to self care, develop, and thrive. These patterns of communication are identifiers that predict growth in each person and the sustainability of positive self esteem. When both partners embody a sense of self esteem plus the encouragement of their partners, we would forecast a greater likelihood of satisfaction and well being in the relationship.

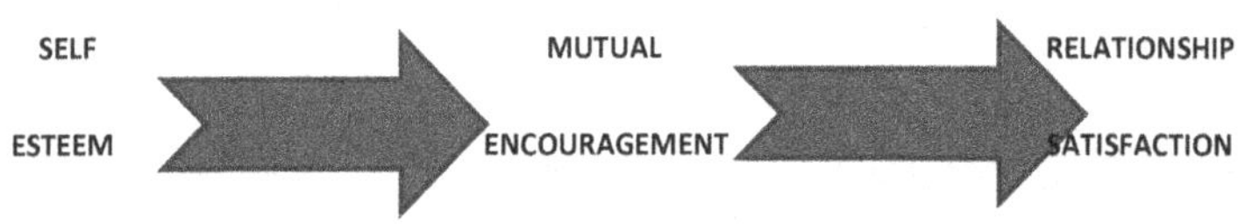

Equals? Fairness? Power Balance?

When we consider the principle of fairness within a relationship, one topic that arises is that of equality. The concept, definition, and measurement of equality could fill volumes. For our purposes, we will examine equality in terms of balance, reciprocity, respect, participation, and contribution.

As we have pondered the respect of individual differences, we have looked to the alternative identifier of "different" as opposed to "right or wrong." We could similarly discuss the notion of equality in terms of: Different methods of contributing, varying modes of participating, and evolving actions to create and maintain balance within a relationship. Yet this is hard.

With the note to the word "evolving," we recognize that you are an evolving figure, so too is the other person in the relationship an evolving figure. If we combine those two figures, then we seem to have a third evolving entity that includes two separately moving parts. Should we add anything else to this contraption, things could get complicated.

Consider your relationship and your own evolution. From the outset, you likely aspired to grow and develop as an individual. The standing from which you entered the relationship was most likely somewhat different from the stance of your partner. You may have discussed the differences and considered them interesting. The differences may have been related to personal background, education, skills, career, or something else. You each likely had your own self perceptions and ambitions for the future. The two of you may have dialogued about your individual goals and prediction forecasts, as well as your existing statuses.

We would expect that your relationship, if healthy, began with a tone of advocacy for one another's pursuits and accomplishments and mutual shouldering of any blows or disappointments. This process may have continued for a while. Over time, it may have changed. Think about these phases of change.

- If there was an unevenness going into your relationship, did this persist proportionately? Did things change?
- If your partner was developing or growing did you view this as positive? Likewise, if you were developing or growing, did your partner celebrate this? Was there conflict therein?
- Was there an inequity in perceived status of any demographic? This could include age, family background, nationality, perceived intelligence, skills, education, career, income, religion, or another identifier.

Vignette:

Steven: I won't be home tonight – it's easier to stay in the city. Got a meeting in the morning too.

Julie: I can't believe this. We talked about this last weekend.

Steven: It can't be helped. Don't be melodramatic over one night. I'll be home tomorrow night.

Julie: (*Silence.*)

Steven: Jules. Jules?

Julie: What?

Steven: I said, I'll be home tomorrow night.

Julie: I hope so, but that's what you told me last week. It's gotten to the point that.... No, never mind. It doesn't matter.

Steven: Please don't pull this. This is totally out of my control. I've got to see clients tonight. You remember how it is. You've just been out of it too long so...

Julie: (*Interrupting*) Are you *kidding* me? It does not help me at all to hear your patronizing tone. *You* were the one who wanted me to cut back. *I'm* the one whose career was cut short.

Steven: (*Silence.*)

Julie: Yeah, no fun to hear the truth. I'll just keep doing my trivial little consulting projects and you just...

Steven: *(Interrupting)* I never said that your consulting was trivial.

Julie: Your actions do when you lord it over me that you're so busy and *I've* forgotten what it's like.

Steven: Jules, c'mon.

Julie: No, you just see the clients and I'll see you when you're all done in a few days. I've got a lot of thinking to do.

Steven: (*Silence, then,*) I'll see if Phil can cover for me.

Julie: No, no, no, don't martyr your way out. I'll be fine. See you. (*Click.*)

What happened?

Julie and Steven met through mutual colleagues. Julie was a newcomer to the industry, Steven was a decade up the ladder. Julie's professional status rose quickly and the couple celebrated her success as they were clinking glasses at their wedding reception. Steven was proud and glowing over his new bride joking with colleagues that she could be a fierce competitor someday. Another five years passed when Julie gave birth to their first child. A nanny came on board for a couple of years until another child emerged. It was challenging juggling career and home, so the couple increased their home size and Julie reduced her workload. She continued working remotely for a while but ultimately felt that her work quality was suffering. The mutual decision was made for Julie to take two years off until their eldest child was in school. The plan was for Julie to continue her intermittent consulting work and begin fostering an entrepreneurial idea that she had hatched in business school.

It seemed a reasonable plan. It could have worked. Yet the unevenness of the relationship seemed to surface – or re-surface. Julie had been attracted to Steven for many reasons. He seemed a man of the world with a top notched education and a family background to match. She grew to love and respect him as he seemed to genuinely care about his colleagues and looked out for them. Steven was impressed with Julie's tenacity as she had put herself through business school and clearly connected with clients as she had a gut sense of people. He bragged to colleagues that her rapport building skill was in her DNA. As Julie transitioned from her corporate role to consulting -- alongside her parenting responsibilities -- Steven felt the connection between them shifted. It was hard to know what caused what. From Steven's view, Julie seemed more concerned about the children's activities than their time together. He felt every spare minute she had was spent researching her business idea. What used to be viewed as an appealing skill set in nurturing client relationships was now disseminated to children, moms, and trademark and patent attorneys.

Julie knew that Steven was displeased. She grew to resent him. She felt he had married her for her bright star, up-and-coming image in the corporate world. Now that she was less involved in corporate culture she felt that the "man of the world" status was now simple superiority and elitism. It was distasteful to Julie. Her disappointment and pain came across as frustration, irritability, and sarcasm. Rather than taking a step back to examine the greater context of their relationship, the couple grew more distant and distrustful leading ultimately to their dissolution.

What Is Fair?

Perhaps most humans would attest that fairness is a priority in their lives. It may be a guiding force, a foot stomping desire, a reason to join a protest, a justification for loving the unlovable, or a rationalization for not loving someone. It is an interesting principle as most humans desire it and can agree on its relevance yet there is vast divergence in how fairness is embodied.

In your past relationship, were you fair? Was your partner fair? Were you fair to others? Were others fair to you as an individual or fair to the two of you? If there was a lack of fairness, why was this? How can people treat each other unfairly when they believe in the principle of fairness?

It is certainly a dilemma.

Couples usually agree that they desire fairness in their relationship. In the introduction of the relationship, often fairness is optimal. Typically, the early phases of our relationships are more focused on what the other person values. We are interested, we marvel at the uniqueness of our partner, and we aim to serve that uniqueness. This may be served with interest, compassion, helpfulness, money, and other resources of time, attention, and deference.

But this can change.

What happens when we begin perceiving the individual differences as:

Boring?

Annoying?

Time consuming?

Expensive?

Troublesome?

Unattractive?

Loud?

Unimportant?

Silly?

Offensive?

Provoking?

Tiring?

Odd?

Unenlightening?

Exhausting?

[Space for you to continue your list]

What to do?

Initially, couples may attempt to comply with their partner's differing preferences, behaviors, or philosophies. Yet conflict may occur as fundamental principles are challenged. If one person perceives dishes in the sink to be normalcy yet the other finds them to be distasteful, then the topic of fairness may be challenged as well as principles of respect, trust, and perspective taking. If one person tends to "win" battles of fairness, this power swing may unhinge the stability of the relationship, particularly if the "winner's" power is a symbol of a deeper inequality. Researchers of equality in relationships have found that a healthy relationship is enhanced by the respect and consideration of what the other partner values, the encouragement of the counterpart's health and well being, and the capacity to adapt to change. These elements have a critical identifier for predicting thriving relationships: *This identifier? Having an equal power balance* (Knudson-Martin, 2013.) Couples benefit from examining and re-examining each person's role as a contributor and participant. As the home and environment evolve, areas of contribution will likely change. Each partner has a personal responsibility to assess and evaluate individual areas of contribution and readjust methods of participating in the relationship and home.

Vignette:

Dory: What IS this?!

Dave: Huh?

Dory: DAVE!

Dave: WHAT?

Dory: What is this in the sink?

Dave: Hmmm.. looks to me like dishes.

Dory: You are disgusting.

Dave: Good.

Dory: You really don't care do you?

Dave: About what?

Dory: You don't care one bit about me.

Dave: Okay, you've gone from showing me something in the kitchen to drama queen land.

Dory: You know how much I hate this.

Dave: (*Ignoring.*)

Dory: Dave.

Dave: (*Staring at the TV.*)

Dory: You really don't care. I've said the exact same thing so many times and you just ignore it.

Dave: Then why don't you stop saying it.

Dory: I can't believe you. I only ask that you think about what matters to me. Just think. But you know what matters and you just do whatever *you* want. So you're telling me you just don't care about what I care about.

Dave: What does it matter if I use the kitchen? I live here you know.

Dory: I'm not saying that you can't use the kitchen. I'm just saying that I can't stand it when I walk into the kitchen I just cleaned and find a sink filled with grimy dishes and things. You promised me that you would clean up after yourself.

Dave: I'll get to them.

Dory: You never will.

Dave: Never is a long time.

Dory. (*Tearfully.*) How can you not see what I'm saying? I mean, when you leave the dishes in there when you know it really upsets me, you're either telling me that you don't care or you're telling me that you expect me to clean up your mess. I hate this.

Dave: (*Silence.*)

Dory: Never mind. I don't care what you do. I don't care at all. You absolutely don't care about me any more. (*Whisks out of the room throwing a towel across the sink.*)

What happened?

So many factors seem to have been influenced: Fairness is one principle debated along with respect, perspective taking, and honoring commitment. It is so easy to slide into all or nothing reasoning in escalating dialogues. While realistically we know that it is difficult to do anything all of the time or none of the time, we tend to pull this card when we are frustrated and feeling accused or mistreated. The child in us ventures down the road of absolute thinking and our fact finding falls away. Mini traumas may be kitchen episodes such as Dave and Dory experienced, yet even a small trauma leads us to quickly defend what we perceive to be right or wrong. The middle ground seems lost and the grey area seems out of sight.

When fairness is the principle challenged in a dialogue, it may be helpful to speak out the principle rather than point to the affront of it. If Dory had noted that she knows Dave is a fair person, she would be emphasizing the principle rather than the undermining of fairness.

As you self observe patterns of dialoguing, it is helpful to pay attention to the negative content from the standpoint of the positive principle that the negatives are undermining. By balancing out the conveyance of positives and negatives, the tone and emotions may be better regulated. Had Dory taken a moment to regulate her emotions, the facts of her message may have been more discernible to Dave. Emotional regulation helps with most dialogues, particularly those conversations that feature a concern about another person's words or actions. When emotions are regulated, then the aberration from the positive may be better addressed.

By emphasizing the positive principle, you will be reminding the person that you believe in his or her capacity to enact positive behavior. The anomaly may then be referenced as noteworthy due to its deviation from the majority of that person's behavior. Dory might have framed her message as, "I know you're a fair guy, so I just get caught off guard when it seems that you're not considering my viewpoint." This would potentially give Dave the opportunity to focus on a positive principle with which he is characteristically aligned.

Review Exercise:

- Stop – regulate breath – regulate emotions – regulate thoughts.
- Consider the negative action – what is it undermining?
- State in your mind the positive that is being undermined.

- Lead the dialogue with the positive noting that ordinarily your partner enacts that positive action.
- Articulate that you believe that it is not the person's intent to undermine that positive principle.

Mutual Respect and Trust

Throughout relationship research, the variable of respect is noted as a predictor of relationship sustainability (Gravningen, et al, 2017.) Consider the interactive process of mutual respect within your relationship. In any relationship we would generally expect respect to be mutual, at least in theory. Yet we would need to define what respect is to self and other. Then we would need to consider how far reaching respect may extend. A simple definition of respect that captures the relating of two people within a partnership is, "To act in a way which shows that you are aware of someone's rights and wishes." Perry Como also captured the spirit of respect in the lyric, "To do what other folks hold dear," (Benjamin & Weiss, 1946.) This perspective on respect conveys the ideology of mutual valuing and adapting within an egalitarian partnership.

And as we examined in the discussion of self care, respecting others begins with how we respect ourselves. With a feeling of self respect -- the respect you are giving yourself and receiving from yourself -- there comes an expectation that you will be respected and you will render respect.

Vignette:

Ben: Why don't you want me to go with you tonight?

Suzanne: I didn't say that. I just don't think you'd enjoy it.

Ben: I could decide that for myself.

Suzanne: (*Absentmindedly buttering her toast*) Huh?

Ben: Last time I went with you, you acted weird.

Suzanne: Went where?

Ben: To the happy hour with your teacher friends.

Suzanne: I already told you that I was just feeling anxious about the unannounced visit from the Dean.

Ben: No, you just didn't think that I fit in.

Suzanne: Ben. That is not what I thought. We talked about that.

Ben: No. You told me that I had a chip on my shoulder. That's not talking about anything.

Suzanne: I didn't mean that. I mean, I was trying to say that sometimes you invent things that are just not accurate.

Ben: Kind of like hallucinating?

Suzanne: No, not like hallucinating. We've been over this and not just about the happy hour. I told you that when the Dean showed up unexpectedly, I was a little thrown off. You know that I'm working really hard to become full professor.

Ben: I know, I know.....

(*Silence between the couple.*)

Ben: I don't think I really want to go anyway....

Suzanne: No, you really should. I really want you to be there.

Ben: No, I guess I was just testing you. I feel like a fish out of water with those people anyway. I'll stay home and watch the game....

What happened? Was this a positive exchange?

Ben was a successful contractor having worked his way from apprentice to foreman to general contractor. He and Suzanne met when Ben managed her apartment renovation. Each were divorced with no children -- Ben, just happy to keep busy; Suzanne, a mid career associate professor with efforts focused on publishing, lecturing, and advancing to full professor in the university. While each partner's background was different from the other, their individual approaches were congruent – diligent, conscientious, agreeable, and hardworking. From the beginning, the chemistry had a spark they felt, and the differences in careers were fun to compare. Ben's family was surprised to meet Suzanne yet embraced her into the family. Suzanne had one remaining immediate family member, her brother, with a few distant relatives across the country. When they married, Suzanne emailed her brother who responded within a week or so with a "Congrats!"

Ben initially approached the divergence in careers with his usual easygoing stance. Yet over time, he began to see that what were initially individual differences became more of a separation in the perception of legitimacy. He was never sure if the legitimacy was pertinent to intelligence, education, or social status. Having worked with clients from many walks of life, Ben had not felt intimidated by the careers of anyone he had encountered. Yet in his own home, he began to have a nagging feeling.

In short, Ben began second guessing himself, doubting his own capacity to be respected. While not considering himself thin skinned, Ben developed what he had to admit was a "chip on his shoulder" – and he much disliked the feeling. While Suzanne started to realize that there were problems, she neglected discussing them with Ben as she had her own uncertainties about the perceptions of others. She found herself wanting to protect Ben from stereotypical biases, feeling caught in the middle as she distained the thought of such judgments. Yet Suzanne recognized in herself a guardedness in discussing certain topics with Ben. She did not want to regale him with facts and data from her grant proposals and questioned herself as to why? She began doubting her own capacity to be fair and accepting of individual differences and vacillated between overly compensating with false praise versus avoiding uncomfortable circumstances through distance and silence.

While this couple had fundamental mutual respect, the miscommunication and lack of communication ultimately destabilized accurate and authentic demonstration of respect. While amicably parting, there was wonder in each person's mind if and when the principle of respect was obstructed.

When you reflect on your relationship, consider the topic of respect for individual differences. While respect is likely a prioritized principle for you, it may occasionally be challenging to apply your open and respectful views to your most intimate relationships. Going forward, consider the relevance of respect regarding the people closest to you. Clearly examine any adjustments you make regarding those in your inner sphere. It is ironic that sometimes humans readjust their principles regarding the people who are closest to home.

Response to Externals: When Family or Friends Disrespect

While a partner's family or friends may disapprove or disrespect the relationship, that partner bears the responsibility of managing those forces. Establishing a respectful yet secure decision making foundation signals to external parties an expectation of mutual respect. Those external relationships then have the option to respect the decision, whether or not they agree with the relationship choice. They may not change their views, yet the steadfastness of the decision maker signals internal security. This solidarity may strengthen the couple's unity without being divisive of any tangential relationships. The external relationships then have the opportunity to join the couple in unity without the expectation of uniformity. Conflict is diffused and over time, a perception shift may occur.

In the Ginger Rogers film, *Kitty Foyle* – adapted from Christopher Morley's novel -- the heroine, Kitty falls in love with Philadelphia main liner Wynnwood Strafford, III. The Straffords are from upscale Darby Mills; the Foyles are from Griscom Street – hard working, warm hearted people. Wyn and Kitty impulsively marry leaving the Straffords distressed – how may this girl from Griscom Street integrate with the Strafford family legacy? Recognizing Wyn's plight, Kitty walks away, divorces, and embraces her autonomy and strength. What to do when the married Wyn shows up five years later suggesting that the couple rekindle their love affair in a far away land? Kitty has a decision to make: A dreamlike romance minus marriage, self respect, and the family's respect, or a practical love from her patient and sincere suitor, Dr. Mark. Kitty chooses love and respect.

External influences have a way of disrupting relationships particularly when the couple is wobbly at the foundation. Perhaps Juliet could have told her parents that she, too, had a few concerns regarding her beau, Romeo. With a tone of assurance yet open mindedness, she might have conveyed that she felt confident in pursuing the relationship, yet she would certainly take their suggestions to heart. Might things have ended differently?

Having self awareness and feeling satisfied and secure help predict the viability of your decision making, how you will be perceived by your partner and by external influences, as well as how you may potentially be swayed (Geisler & Alwood, 2015.) Your satisfaction and security may not change the perspectives of others, yet it conveys that you feel good about your perspective, and are making well grounded, informed decisions.

As you think about your past relationship and sort through examples of respect and disrespect, consider these questions:

- Did you respect yourself?
- Did your partner self respect?
- Did you respect your partner?
- Did your partner respect you?
- How could you have changed how you respected your partner?
- How could your partner have changed how he or she respected you?
- Did you and your partner respect the individual differences between one other?
- Do you believe that you have a fundamental respect of individual differences? Consider how you do or do not.
- Did you respect the people in your partner's life?

- Did your partner respect the people in your life?
- Were external relationships an influencing factor in your relationship?
- Were the ground rules of respect discussed? Did they change? Were they revisited?

Mutual Trust

Definitions of the principle of trust include: A firm belief in the reliability, truth, ability, and strength of someone or something; having confidence, faith, certainty, assurance, conviction, and reliance. Lewicki, McAllister, and Bies (1998) defined trust as "an individual's belief in, and willingness to act on the basis of, the words, actions, and decisions of another." Many researchers and theorists have hypothesized that an individual's attachment style has significant influence on how securely trust is established (Hazan & Shaver, 1987.)

Trust seems to be one of the most powerful influences in any relationship.

At some point in your past relationship, you and your partner likely acknowledged the importance of trust. You may have agreed that it is vital to a relationship's health and sustainability. Consider the role of trust in your relationship. Take some time to write out your thoughts regarding the following questions:

How do you define trust?
How was trust defined in your relationship?
Was trust discussed?
Was distrust a source of conflict?
Did you trust your partner?
Did your partner trust you?

The Study of Trust

Relationship studies have found that distrust is not solely the absence of trust. Rather, it is having a negative expectation of another person that generates distrust. This expectation of negativity may be influenced by perceived inconsistencies in a person's actions as well as in discrepancies between the person's fundamental values and behavior. For example, a person may at times demonstrate trustworthy behavior, yet at other times behavior is erratic and questionable. Envision a friend who tells you she will meet you on the corner every Friday at noon yet only shows up 40% of the time. Would you trust her more if this percentage was 95%? Trust is also negatively affected by incongruities between beliefs and actions. Imagine a man who says he has strong convictions regarding trust. Later you see him flirting with a woman in a bar as he is leaving a message for his wife regarding his working late at the office.

Contrastingly, having consistent expectations of positive actions within a relationship predicts a positive perception of mutual trust. When a partner observes a consistent pattern of trustworthy behavior in his or her counterpart over a period of time, the expectation of trust becomes normalized. This consistency preserves the partner's self esteem and solidifies his or her belief in the counterpart's capacity to be trustworthy.

Then how may trust be rebuilt when it is compromised? Let's look more closely at different forms of trust. *Calculus based trust* is a form of trust which is broadly perceived most relevant to professional relationships. This mode of trust has application to personal relationships as well. Calculus based trust is strengthened by generating patterns of interaction that are constant, reliable, and predictable. Methods of implementation may include establishing goals, timelines, and consequences with mutual monitoring of the process. This process generates consistency which evolves a feeling of safety within the relationship.

Within personal relationships, mutual trust is supported when *identification based trust* is nurtured. This form of trust is *influenced by the emotions* of each individual. The *values and perceptions* of each person affect the development of identification based trust. When each person respects both common and dissimilar facets of the other's identity, trust is enhanced. Sensitivity and responsiveness to a partner's goals, motivations, and personal interests further develop identification based trust (Lewicki & Wiethoff, 2000.)

Midnight Vignette:

Trudy: (*Turning on the light and tapping her husband*) Stan..... (*Silence*) Stan?!

Stan: (*Mumbling*) What?

Trudy: I can't stop thinking about this dream I've had.

Stan: (*Sighing*) Which dream?

Trudy: The one where you leave me.

Stan: Trudy. Can't this wait until morning?

Trudy: No, I just can't sleep.

Stan: Is this the dream where you come home and all of my things are gone?

Trudy: Yes.

Stan: Well, it's a dream. You're awake now. My things are here and so I am. Goodnight. (*Rolling over.*)

Trudy: Stan! No. You've got to talk with me.

Stan: (*Resignedly*) Okay. Let's talk.

Trudy: Why did you marry me?

Stan: What?

Trudy: No, I mean if you really think about it, it doesn't make sense – why did you marry me?

Stan: I don't know. I mean, okay, we met and got along really well and we like being together.

Trudy: (*Silence.*)

Stan: And I love you.

Trudy: But how do I know that's enough?

Stan: Babe...... how does anybody know much of anything.

Trudy: I think you've started to get tired of me. You just don't seem to want to do things with me anymore.

Stan: That's not true. We're just both busy.

Trudy: No, you used to always make time for us. Now we go out maybe once or twice a month.

Stan: Okay. So we'll start going out more.

Trudy: That's not enough.

Stan: What?! Look, you're just setting me up here. What do you want me to say?

Trudy: That you would never never leave me. I don't think I could take it.

Stan: Trudy – everybody has to know that they'd be okay on their own. But that doesn't mean I'm going to leave you.

Trudy: I think we should get some counseling.

Stan: Why?

Trudy: I think someone needs to help us make our relationship stronger.

Stan: Huh? So that they'll make sure that I don't leave you? What if you decide to leave me?

Trudy: I'd never do that.

Stan: How could I know that?

Trudy: Because you can trust me.

Stan: And you don't trust me?

Trudy: I don't know. I don't think I trust me.

Stan: What's that supposed to mean?

Trudy: I don't think I trust myself that I'd be ok if you weren't here.

Stan: (*Sigh.*)

What happened here?

While Trudy was able to openly express her fears, she struggled to identify and discuss their origin. Seeking counseling was a viable option for deciphering the root of her concerns. Yet Stan felt penalized by Trudy's insecurities. He was reticent to tell Trudy that he believed that she did not trust his commitment to her based on her prior relationship's conflicts. When he had previously mentioned her broken engagement, Trudy had cried for an hour and shouted that she did not want to talk about that relationship ever again. Stan knew that he loved her and did not intend to leave yet he was tiring of what he perceived as an insatiable need for reassurance from his spouse.

Most humans have the potential to go a little overboard at times; the capacity to trust is no exception to this propensity. In therapy we often say, "Trust is about *trusting yourself* to take the worst of the world." If clients catastrophize about relationship distrust, we then test the hypothesis. We explore a hypothetical catastrophe of the worst case scenario. We try to define what the worst trust calamity could be. Then we question, "What is the likelihood that the worst form of distrust will happen in your relationship?" Typically, the response is that people have generally been trustworthy in their lives, therefore, it is neither logical nor statistically probable that a distrust catastrophe will occur. This process helps manage the human tendency to focus on the negative in the more accurate presence of predominately positive data.

In therapy we occasionally puzzle over the demonstration of "old data" – meaning past experiences – onto current circumstances. Psychological theorists refer to this process as generalization or selective abstraction – taking an isolated incident and generalizing it to other similar circumstances. Generalization may be recognized when the current partner is receiving the distrust felt for a prior partner. It is all too easy to apply a consequence meant for a past circumstance to that of the present. Yet this is an inaccurate tool for the present job. It is even more puzzling to the receiver when the present tool is meant for an accumulation of "past jobs" leaving the present person feeling slugged with a sledge hammer meant for a group of other people (Dymond, et al, 2015.)

As we have examined, trust is developed over time through reliability, perspective taking, authentic interest in the other person's values, and sensitivity to one other's preferences. And if trust is undermined, it must be reestablished and rebuilt over time. For some relationships, this principle is the most vulnerable and takes the longest to strengthen. There is little substitute for time and consistency when we are developing or rebuilding the principle of trust.

Consistency generally creates a feeling of safety. For many, safety is an important part of the experience of love. Perhaps this desire for consistency and safety comes in part from the child within us.

Parenting workshops and childrearing literature emphasize the importance of consistency – consistency in demonstrating unconditional love to a child, having consistent boundaries, having consequences that are commensurate with the affront and being consistent therein, having consistent routines and schedules, and having a consistent tone and demeanor in speaking with the child. It makes sense that adults, as former children, would appreciate consistency. As children, we would have developed some anxiety if our parents had intermittently cared for us or told us, "Remember that one time I fed you," or "Don't forget that I took you to the dentist a few years ago," or "I told you I loved you when you were born." Reinforcement of positive behavior is also more beneficial when there is consistency. Intermittent reinforcement tends to make humans anxious – children and adults -- and sometimes predicts that the person will give up on the reinforcer altogether (Bloomfield, et al, 2004.)

A primary basis of consistency is honesty. Honesty refers to truth telling as well as to honesty of tone. It is difficult for a listener to believe a message of love when the tone bears a ring of disdain. Having honesty and consistency in tone is two-fold: The person's tone is consistent over time and the person's tone is consistent with the nature of the relationship. If the relationship is loving and respectful, then the tone has a tone of love and respect. And this tone is pervasively heard throughout the relationship's interactions. Similarly, truth-telling is more believable when used consistently. Discrepancies in honesty leave the recipient questioning the past, present, and future.

Vignette:

Polly was curled up in the corner of the sofa, anxiously biting her thumbnail. Why didn't he call? Ugh. Sporadic texting is so annoying. Why was Sam so consistent in his communication when they were *first* dating? And now there were spotty texts of "hi!" and "sure no worries" and "cool."

What had once been a great banter had turned into cryptic shorthand communications with lengthy lags and sometimes days of no contact.

What did those silences mean? Why did she feel so upset so much of the time? Why couldn't she stop thinking about him?

Polly's therapist reminded her that the interpretation of silence is a dangerous thing. Yet this seemed different. What was he *thinking?* And then: *Jubilation. Phone Buzzed with text,* "POLL! Let's meet at 8!" Polly's response: "Great. Can't wait!"

Polly sprang into action though still not knowing what they would be doing and where. Her freelance writing would have to wait. She was going for a mani-pedi. Grab keys, phone, and bag and...

...then at the door Polly halted. "No way. I'm not falling for it this time." She pulled her phone out and wrote, "Nix that. Project's due. Raincheck." *Send.* In 30 seconds, "Bummed. You'll nail the project! CU!"

Polly fell onto the sofa, face first. "Aggghhhhh! What have I *done*?!"

While Polly's exaggeration could be categorized as strategic game playing, hers was an understandable response to Sam's inconsistency. Relationship building has new tools in online dating and multiple forms of electronic communication yet with these tools come some obstacles and complexities.

When you consider your past relationship, you may recall some ups and downs that we could normalize. As well, you may also remember inconsistencies in communication and general demeanor. These inconsistencies may have devolved from annoyance and confusion to insecurity and pain. What might be characterized as simple shifts in emotions could escalate to more volatile mood swings in one or both partners. Couples who have volatility in areas of mutual respect, consideration, and empathy tend to struggle when they are on the downward spiral. And when demeanor is on an intensely high level, there is ultimate tension from the unsustainable high.

Consistency may be perceived as drab and boring. However, consistency in doing anything – including being who you are -- tends to help humans "get better" at what they are doing. In contrast to relationship volatility, when you are consistent in the treatment of your partner, your consistency line is a rising line. You are refining your outgoing energy and you are developing and nurturing your communication patterns. This is how relationships deepen in their connections and their interactions become enriched and ultimately embody a natural sustainable ease (Campbell, et al, 2010.)

Vignette:

For the first time in her relationship, Barb experienced what she admitted was fear. She was not fearing that Phil would physically harm her, yet the tension in her face and rigidity in her body informed her thoughts that she was anxious for Phil to come home that evening. She had hurried her work commute as much as she could so that she could arrive home first to tidy the apartment and look through the fridge for dinner options. Yet she realized that she was actually just wanting 15 minutes of peace and quiet before Phil walked in the door.

Barb recognized this feeling from her childhood though her mom had squelched the idea that she had feared

Dad's homecoming each weeknight. She had called it, "prevention time" as she scurried around getting ready for his arrival. Barb recalled that Dad was a ritualistic person with a frequent after work stop at his favorite bar to "cool down," and a habitual call from the bar before his short commute from train station to the house. He typically asked who would be home for dinner and how much trouble had the kids gotten into at school that day. He would be irritated if any of the kids were gone and annoyed if dinner was going to be leftovers. Mom had always said that Dad set the thermostat for the night. If he was jolly from everything going his way, it would be a smooth night. If his hardnosed boss had barked that day, the kids had better lay low.

Barb tried to chuckle at the similarities between her father and Phil yet found her breathing more difficult and her head began to throb. Their story was different from Mom and Dad's as each had demanding jobs and similarly taxing pressure. Yet Barb managed her stressors through fitness and occasional yoga classes and

Phil opted for alcohol and TV. When work ran smoothly, he was lots of fun and would call Barb at the office suggesting that they meet for dinner after work. Barb loved a glass of wine too, but Phil lacked an off switch when it came to drinking. Sometimes Barb didn't know what was more anxiety producing – coming home after a night out or hoping that a night at home for dinner would be relaxing and enjoyable rather than tense and explosive.

Inconsistency in mood and tone tends to generate anxiety. When you have a relationship that is unpredictable, you are at risk of developing anticipatory anxiety – a chronic, vigilant expectancy of something negative. Even when you think about the person, your heart may begin racing, your palms become clammy, your breathing shortens. Think about it: Your phone rings. The name that flashes on your phone is that person in your life who is volatile and unpredictable. Sometimes he's on the top of the world. Other times his tone is explosive, matching a mood of anger and aggression. Think about how you feel as you are about to say, hello? Which version of himself will he be? Will the conversation be a mini-trauma? (Simpson, et al, 2001.)

Now think about a person in your life who is steady and generally consistent. How do you feel when that person's name pops up on your phone or shows up in your email inbox? True, you may take that person for granted, yet the consistent tone and steady behavior builds a sense of trust and safety over time. Trust and safety, along with honesty and esteem predict the health and well being of a relationship with anyone. And intimacy, power, and competence are positively influenced by the reduction of trauma in our existence – even mini-traumas (Beck and Clark, 2010).

Writing Exercise – Going forward:

As you reflect on your past relationship and consider the topic of consistency, it may be helpful to visualize the consistent steady line that you *now* desire in your relationships – in tone and demeanor, actions, and lifestyle. What do you feel is sustainable?

Think about what you would like your life to be day to day.

How would you describe your preferred lifestyle and quality of life? Consider the pace of living that is most comfortable for you.

What do you find most fulfilling in your life?

What activities do you find satisfying and enjoyable?

It is not too much to ask of someone to be the same person every day. Despite having a cold or a sprained ankle, you remain the same person. You may not have your average physical stamina, yet you retain the capacity to be who you fundamentally are. Flexibility and openness to new experiences are predictors of psychological well being. Nonetheless, this flexibility does not imply that any form of abuse is acceptable. An abruptly shifting negative or demeaning tone is not essential when circumstances or situations are down. In crisis, it is each person's responsibility to emotionally self regulate. A mantra in crisis intervention training is, "Don't become the crisis." While day to day experiences have many variants, it is possible to retain your sense of self, even when crisis strikes.

With societal sexual norms continuously shifting come inevitable conflicts. Many are concerned about the implications of this shift, some are confused, others delighted, and some choose hibernation as their best response.

A therapy office is an unusual room. It is one in which people tend to examine topics that they do not necessarily discuss over coffee or across the family dinner table. It is a setting that emphasizes confidentiality and trust. These principles are honored; respect of individual differences is assured; unconditional positive regard is consistently present; all confidences are preserved and sheltered. Yet long before a client becomes a client and an appointment is secured, physical intimacy concerns are frequently presented as a subject to unravel. Some people are concerned about media pressure. Others are conflicted about pressuring and comparing. And some are struggling from receiving pressure. But if a person is considering a relationship connection, it is likely that intimacy is on the mind.

If you are reflecting on the physical intimacy aspect of your relationships, you are not alone. And doesn't it make sense? Many forms of intimacy are part of a healthy human existence. How humans connect with others is influenced by many variables. If we are each evolving and developing as individuals, we would expect that these evolutionary processes would not occur in synchronization – even with your intimate partner. Variables enter our development and alter our course. These variables may include:

Self perception of image

Others' perceptions of image

Health

Medications

Work environment and stressors

Children

Family and family stressors

Home environment

Fitness

Aging

Hormones

Other people

Books

Movies

Television

Internet & social media detractors

The list goes on. Yet perception of self may lead the list in how we perceive our own physical intimacy habits and patterns.

Self View

Not surprisingly, when humans view themselves positively, they set themselves up for what happens next. If your self view is positive, then you tend to enter into your world with the expectation that you will encounter people who will also view you positively. Alternatively, if your self view is or becomes negative, then you are more likely to expect that others will concur with your negative view. Self perception regarding intimacy may follow a similar pattern. How you perceive yourself as an intimate partner may be influenceable by many variables. And many of those variables may at times feel out of your control.

Vignette:

Mark: So is there something wrong with you?

Darla: What's THAT supposed to mean?

Mark: Let's face it – you've changed. When we were first together, you couldn't keep your hands off me. Now, you make every excuse to avoid me. What's the deal?

Darla: Well, if that's your way of being attractive, then look in the mirror.

Mark: So THAT'S it. You don't like how I look?

Darla: NO, idiot. I mean, just listen to yourself. What do you mean, "What's the deal?"

Mark: I mean, there needs to be a lot more going on around here other than my driving people to and from the train station. I'm sick of just being the janitor and everyone's servant.

Darla: Ok, are we talking about intimacy or are we talking about how long suffering you are as a husband and father.

Mark: Oh, never mind. You don't get it.

Darla: Don't just walk away from me.

Mark: I'd better or I'll say something you won't want to hear. A guy needs more than just being a servant or a handyman. I'm out of here.

Darla held herself back as she found herself wanting to follow Mark down the stairs. Yet in many ways, she agreed with him. It wasn't that she did not find him attractive, yet Darla recognized she did not find herself attractive any more. Or at least, she felt that she had no interest in any form of intimacy. Her gynecologist had skimmed over the influence of hormonal changes, yet Darla felt that the extra fifteen pounds that she had put on were much more of a problem. She had read in a women's magazine that libido might decline somewhere in her 40s or 50s, yet she thought that she was just burned out and intimacy was no longer that important....

...Mark plopped himself into the driver's seat and turned the ignition. As he pulled the gear shift, he paused before pressing the gas. He thought to himself,

Where am I really going? I mean, I'm just running away again, like Darla says. But she's just different now... I don't think it's me. The urologist said I'm totally fine..... just normal aging..... But I'm way too young to be living like a monk...... Tom's found that girl from the office and told me to go for it. But I'm not into that. If that's what it takes for me to feel young again, well......

Mark did not genuinely want to consider leaving the marriage and could not imagine himself having an affair. He felt that something needed to change yet he did not know where to start. Darla actually had similar thoughts as Mark in being conflicted about her lackluster feelings and thought occasionally about moving out and living alone. It would be quiet and Darla could try to find herself.

Yet Darla's mind heard the alarm bells peal when the principal at her son's high school paid extra attention to her. She thought, *What in the world? Oh my gosh. I don't know what just went through my mind. I've got to pull it together. I am not that kind of person and never have been. But I can't believe how good it felt to have someone compliment me and respect my work on the school board.... Mark hasn't used that tone in more than five years.....*

What happened here? What to do?

So many things. Darla and Mark had multiple concerns that appeared to have an origin of negative self views. While communication lacked mutual respect and honesty, each partner was struggling with his and her interpretation of what the concerns were. Darla was detracted by body image and waved away her doctor's thoughts on hormonal changes. She believed that she had lost the basic desire for intimacy -- until the principal paid attention in a way that resonated with her. Mark's concerns were blurry as he feared having sexual dysfunction as his older brother had experienced. Yet he found fault in Darla while simultaneously feeling rejected. He began comparing her to other women in his office believing that they would be more likely to ignite a spark.

Attribution Theory – How does this theory apply to intimacy?

"Attribution theory deals with how the social perceiver uses information to arrive at causal explanations for events. It examines what information is gathered and how it is combined to form a causal judgment" (Fiske, & Taylor, 1991).

As you consider your past relationship, it may be helpful to contemplate the role of intimacy alongside the self views that you and your partner had. It is not uncommon for couples to misattribute the source of a changing or diminishing libido. While you could easily decide that you no longer have an interest in intimacy based on who you are, you could just as easily decide that the source of your dulling desire is your partner. As with most components of a relationship, self awareness is a critical first step followed by accurate fact checking. You will be better equipped to make an informed decision if you have researched your topic. Think about any intimacy changes that may have occurred in your relationship. What do you believe was the cause of the effect? Is it possible that one person's self view change was attributed to the other person?

Clashes Between Emotional Intimacy and Physical Intimacy

It is not unusual to hear a partner's frustration that physical intimacy did not occur. Interestingly, it is also not unusual to hear a partner remark, "I don't know what's wrong with her. Just because we fought, she slept on the couch. I mean, c'mon! What gives?"

Let's try to answer the man's inquiry of "What gives?" When his partner is disinclined to consent to physical intimacy post-argument, we would predict that she did not feel that negative interpersonal emotions correlate with positive physical intimacy. Her feelings may be influenced by many factors and beliefs, both past and present. Attribution theory suggests that her feelings may be influenced by:

- A consensus with past experiences in her memory and awareness
- How she feels people *should* address intimacy and conflict
- What she *typically* chooses to do in such a circumstance (Kelley, 1967.)

In other words, his partner is thinking, "What the *heck*? I can't stand it when guys want intimacy even after a fight! It is TOTALLY wrong to want to sleep with me after you disrespected me. I NEVER sleep in the same room with a guy who berates me!" Research further supports the theory that anger, frustration, and anxiety may have informed her thoughts and emotions leading her to deduce that physical intimacy was not desired (Lang,

1994.) While one person may be more prone to disengaging mind and emotions from the body, another may more resolutely associate mind and body when psychologically distressed.

- When you consider the evolution of physical intimacy in your past relationship, what was your view of the link between emotional intimacy and physical intimacy? What was your partner's view?
- Can one exist without the other? Is it possible to separate emotional intimacy from physical intimacy?

There is not an absolute answer to these inquiries. We would expect that the development of a healthy committed relationship would include many forms of emotional intimacy. Ultimately if that relationship persisted, we would predict that physical intimacy would likely occur. While one may exist without another – in a mutually consenting sexual relationship or in an emotionally intimate relationship without physical intimacy -- we would be likely to correlate physical intimacy with emotional intimacy within a committed partnership.

Viewing Changes as Opportunities Not Obstacles

As two people in a relationship evolve, the transitions and changes may initially be perceived as challenges. Yet changes in emotions, thoughts, and physiological phenomena have the potential to be opportunities for exploring intimacy alternatives within the relationship. For some, this could be less physical intimacy leading to more emotional intimacy. Others may see that more time and freedom have a yield of deeper emotional intimacy and a correlating increase in physical intimacy.

Changes in a relationship may initially be perceived as wrong or frightening. Yet change need not be viewed as negative – change is just different. Ultimately, changes in intimacy may be viewed as different forms of connecting within the relationship. Through open, positive communication, couples have a mutual opportunity to develop their relationship's intimacy at all levels, even in the presence of change.

Your Partner Is Not a Mind Reader - Your Partner May Be More Interested Than You Think

In the 1957 film, *An Affair to Remember*, Cary Grant and Deborah Kerr exchanged quips that implied that they could read one another's thoughts. It was an endearing and romantic element of their evolving relationship. Yet even in this fictitious love story, the lovers could not read the other's mind and miscommunication nearly separated them forever. As you contemplate your past relationship, recall the times when you or your partner may have fallen into the mind reading trap – you may have been the trapper or the trapped. While it is great fun to believe that we may read one another's thoughts, there is little substitute for simple and direct communication of thoughts and preferences – with respect to intimacy and all else.

Your Self Worrying May Be Perceived as Rejection

Looking back at Mark and Darla's communication, it is notable that Mark perceived Darla's negative self view as rejection. While Darla may have had greater interest in physical intimacy if Mark had been more attentive or sensitive, she was inadvertently overlooking Mark's own negative self doubt and his ultimate feeling of rejection.

Catching Flies?

Had Mark taken a more positive approach in re-establishing an emotional connection with Darla, he might have extended to her a more intriguing and appealing message of good news. Rather, he was inadvertently projecting a less desirable negative view rather than conveying the positive reasons for his desire for intimacy. Had either partner commenced with an expression of appreciation, interest, and love for the other, the perception would have been clearer that they were each viewed as attractive, interesting, and lovable. While catching flies with honey may seem a form of trickery, if you are first considering the reasons why you love and are attracted to your partner, you are increasing the likelihood that your expression will be considered a report of good news rather than one of negative propaganda.

Individual Differences and Preferences

Within healthy, well functioning relationships, there are countless stories of physical intimacy. These stories may vary substantially from one couple to another or evolve within the relationship of one couple. There are experiences of awakening, transformation, love, and trust that may have a yield of respect for transitioning individual preferences and differences. This evolving process is a healthy one when communication and relatedness is mutually respectful, trust filled, fair, empathic, and honest.

Your memories may be clouded or harsh regarding the intimate part of your past relationship. Yet you have an opportunity to bring forward the discoveries and growth and leave behind the limitations, disappointments, and pain. Going forward, you have the chance to derive benefit from your history of physical intimacy. With the empowerment of experience, you have erudite wisdom to commit to your potential future intimacy journey. While the principal's interest may have been intriguing to Darla simply because it was new and different, perhaps your future may be viewed as a new and different summer of opportunities in relating to others. These relations may have a range of intimate connections – connecting emotionally, physically, or a little of both.

Throughout these writings we have examined fundamental identifiers that help predict the health in your relationships. And throughout we have interwoven a critical thread: Talk with your partner. And listen to each other. And think about *how* you talk and listen.

The concept of "communication" has many definitions and derivatives. Yet the overarching element is the idea of *connecting two entities*. We could swiftly subdivide communication into two categories of verbal and nonverbal. Yet when we further examine communication, we must explore the energy underneath it such as motivation, methods of forming messages, methods of receiving and decoding messages, interpreting and making sense of communication, retention capacity, and managing abstract versus concrete forms of communication. Then we must consider other influences such as modes of communication including visual, auditory, tactile, olfactory, written, and others.

In many relationship studies, researchers have noted the influence of communication in relationships. However, an interesting insight is in the value of happiness and satisfaction in each person who is communicating. As a matter of fact, studies have found that individual satisfaction and happiness may have the greatest influence on the well being of the relationship leading to more positive communication. While the cause and effect aspect is undeniable, it is notable that a relationship may be influenced by each partner's satisfaction as much as by their methods of communication (Lavner, et al, 2016.)

Think about the correlations of satisfaction and communication in your relationship. Do you agree that you may have communicated more effectively and warmly when you were experiencing greater life satisfaction? Do you think it is possible that being happier could have a positive influence on your communication? It certainly seems to have the potential of a chicken or the egg conundrum. This theory concurs with our prior discussion of your self view having direct influence on how you view others and how they view you.

Communication and Conflict

Within many relationships, communication is influenced by *how* individuals approach conflict. Sometimes the manner of addressing conflict becomes a greater obstacle than the original conflict itself. Effective communication applies solution finding skills and assertiveness to the management of conflict. Researchers have identified that the tonality and feeling of hostility and contempt have the tendency to escalate the negatives in communication, thereby negatively influencing conflict. Emotions of warmth and endearment embody a more positive mode of communication which would more likely predict that conflict is neutralized (Kim, et al, 2007.)

Vignette

Tony: You just don't like my family.

Annie: That is TOTALLY untrue. Where in the world do you come up with that?

Tony: All I asked was to take a drive to Aunt Sue's.

Annie: Noooooo, what you *told* me was that if I didn't pack up the twins to drive three hours in the car, then I'm a selfish witch.

Tony: I didn't say that.

Annie: You not only said that but then you threatened to pull the plug and walk. Whatever *that* means!

Tony: (*Silence. Then walking toward the front door.*)

Annie: Tony. If you walk out, I truly can't say if the babies and I will be here when you get back.

Tony: Well, there you go. You're all set to leave when you don't get your way. And THAT'S not selfish?

Annie: Are you kidding me? If *I* don't get my way? What are you TALKING ABOUT?!

Tony: You know that you never have any intention of going to see my family. You just whine and moan about how tired you are. Excuses, excuses.

Annie: I am so tired because I get up every hour to feed one or the other baby. YOU KNOW THAT! (*Pushing Tony's keys and hat to the floor.*)

Tony: (*Mocking*) "I am sooooooo tired." And you said that all you ever wanted was to be a mother.

Annie: (*Turning sharply, causing a stack of diapers to tumble*) GET OUT! You never help me with the twins and you never ever will! (*Tears falling, face flushed and contorted*) I am utterly exhausted and at this moment, I HATE you with everything in me! (*Running from the room.*)

Tony grabs keys and hat and bolts for the door.

Annie: (*Screaming*) GOOD! I hope you never come back! (*Sobbing....... Babies begin to wail.*)

What happened?

Annie was a first time mother of nine month old twins. She was struggling with nursing both babies and was beginning to wonder if she had post partum depression. She had not slept through the night for over nine months as the final trimester of her pregnancy had been uncomfortable and her high risk status had added to her anxiety. She had attempted to speak with Tony about her concerns. When she asked him if she could hire a babysitter to help her throughout the week, Tony had responded that they could not afford a babysitter when he was the only person working. Annie had collapsed into tears. Tony interpreted her reaction as Annie's disappointment in him. He felt that she believed that his job and income were inadequate. *He* felt inadequate. He had bolted from the room. He shouted that his mother had single handedly taken care of four children under the age of six without a single complaint so what was *Annie's* problem?

While confounding variables of fatigue and misinterpretation may have obstructed effective solution finding in Annie and Tony's emotional dialogue, the pre-existing dissatisfaction and unhappiness in each partner may have influenced their capacities to speak rationally and respectfully. Communication with such variables may be difficult regardless of any communication skill set. When physiological and emotional concerns occur such as fatigue and life event changes -- including child bearing, job loss, and illness -- couples may benefit from slowing down dialogues with time and breathing. The "24 hour rule" of awaiting cooler and calmer minds may assist couples in more effective communication. Then a re-assessment of the sources of satisfaction or dissatisfaction may help both people identify what is troubling them. Perhaps a rule of thumb is, if in doubt, acknowledge the person's message, propose a cooling period, and *wait.* As we examined in earlier chapters, by slowing down your breathing and thoughts and calmly assessing your mind and body, your brain functions more efficiently

(Goleman, 1995.) Allowing your executive functioning skills to work, you are better equipped to organize your thoughts and emotions as well as to reduce impulsivity and regulate emotional reasoning. This process may increase the likelihood of having a more rational and productive dialogue.

Think about the communication that you had in your past relationship during highly charged emotional times. Consider how you felt at the time. What do you think could have been done differently? Were there confounding variables such as fatigue? Major life events? Overuse of alcohol? Misinterpretation due to impulsivity?

Stonewalling -- Unacknowledged Words – Emotional Abandonment

If someone exclaims something and is not acknowledged, chances are that the person will repeat the content, perhaps with more enthusiasm; perhaps with more distress. If you yelled into your front hall, "I won the Pulitzer Prize!" and your family stared at you blankly, you would likely try again with, "You *guys*! I won the Pulitzer!!!" We would predict that they would respond favorably, once they heard and understood you. However, if they were feeling usurped by your honor, perhaps their intensity would not match yours. And if you walked in the house and shouted, "Hey! The house is on fire!!!" and your family continued watching TV, you would likely repeat yourself with even greater emphasis. You might even grab a sleeve and say, "Don't you understand me?! *We have to get out*!"

Unacknowledged words tend to create disappointment, feelings of disrespect, and potential conflict. Stonewalling – refusing to respond or engage dialogue – is a form of emotional abandonment. It is sometimes viewed as more cruel than physical abandonment as the person is present yet has chosen to emotionally abandon. Avoidance of any sort is divisive in relationships yet stonewalling has the potential of creating long term emotional scars. Speaking directly with a partner and responding directly may seem more difficult. While stonewalling may seem the path of least resistance, in reality, it conveys at least two messages: 1) You disregard the person; 2) You do not respect the person enough to acknowledge him or her. This may not be how you feel, nonetheless, it is likely that your listener will perceive the action as such.

Go Ahead – Speak Directly

In the 1962 film, *That Touch of Mink*, Cary Grant plays the part of a rich businessman to Doris Day's working girl role, Miss Timberlake. In an awkward board room scene, Cary Grant asks Miss Timberlake what *she* would do about Mr. Benson, a man who would not sell his company when they offered him more than it was worth. The board members defend that they have tried everything – they have talked with Mr. Benson's lawyers, directors, and executive assistant. What else could they do? To which Miss Timberlake innocently asks whether they have talked with *Mr. Benson*? They admit that they have not. Ah, says she – the same thing happened to her Aunt Rachel when her suitor kept sending her marriage proposal letters -- yet Aunt Rachel would not comply. Miss Timberlake notes that Aunt Rachel had actually wanted to get married but she felt that he should have asked her in person. Cary Grant notes that perhaps Mr. Benson is "eager to become a bride but has never been asked…. hmmm, how would Aunt Rachel feel about a phone call?" A guileless Miss Timberlake replies, "No, she wouldn't say yes until he came to the house." He did. And now they have eight children. Grant characteristically quips, "Well, that couldn't have happened over the phone."

An unlikely story perhaps, yet it is notable that speaking directly may be perceived as the more respectful and understandable mode of communication. The yield may not be eight children, yet at least the outcome is not obstructed or misinterpreted through a circuitous route of communication.

Listening

More listening than talking creates a sturdy foundation for fruitful communication. Successful sales people know about listening. They know after a few fiascos that *not listening* can lose them a sale. What if the client told the sales person that she has a fear of water, does not swim, and does not drive yet the sales person is hard selling the pool and the parking garage? What did the sales person miss? It could be the neighborhood preference, the age of the building, the color of the structure, the size of the garden, or who knows what? Listening and reflecting allows some space and time for breathing and reduces human tendencies for impulsivity or knee jerk responses. When we forget to listen, we may miss the tone of the person's words. We may emphasize the wrong part of the picture. We may miss the forest for the trees. We may even miss some good news.

When you reflect on your past relationship consider these communication topics:

Ability to solution find

Assertiveness

Positive and negative tonality

Stonewalling and avoidance tactics

Speaking directly with your partner

Listening

Looking Ahead and Charging Forward

We have looked back to your past relationship and have examined influential areas with an eye on discoveries for your future. As you continue moving forward, hopefully you will be a bit lighter and buoyed as some limitations of the past have been lifted. Moving ahead, you have an opportunity to benefit from the discoveries and strengths that you have mined from the past. Let's take a look at who you are and how you feel.

- Knowing who you are and demonstrating that person is the primary responsibility that you have as a human. It is stabilizing to anchor yourself to your foundational principles. From time to time, remind yourself of your beliefs and what matters the most to you.

- Embracing who you are and consistently being who you are will assist you in your development.

- Cognitive dissonance is that uncomfortable feeling that humans have when their actions and thoughts deviate from what they fundamentally believe.

- Synchronizing your actions with your basic principles will reduce feelings of cognitive dissonance.

Humans are inherently flawed thus we recognize that we will inevitably deviate from our core beliefs. When we feel that uncomfortable cognitive dissonance, then we have a decision to make – do we want to continue the deviation? Or do we want to restore congruity, synchronize our actions with our basic principles, and operate from our sturdy positive foundations?

- Think about what you believe.
- Think about how you demonstrate your beliefs.
- Think about how you feel when you deviate from your basic beliefs.

- This odd, uncomfortable feeling is your cue.
- When you feel that funny feeling of discomfort, aim to look at alternative actions that better fit your foundational principles.

Standing on solid ground is a signal that you are AOK. When you are well anchored to your secure foundation, you need not have defense mechanisms. In fact, there is no need for a defense if you are not wobbly at your foundational level. A wobble tends to suggest to you that you are concerned about something within. When this happens, something inside you tells you that the concern needs to be concealed or protected, thus the defense arises and self protection is demonstrated in some form. This could be a bravado to cover your fear of seeming weak; putting someone down when you want to sound smarter; lying about something in an effort to please someone; or cheating on your work to prevent someone from disapproving. Yet when we remind ourselves that we are human and inherently flawed, we may also remind ourselves that acceptance of our flaws helps to stabilize us. Then we are better equipped to engage with others with less need to erect our defense walls. This relaxes us and tends to relax those around us.

Vignette:

Laurie stood before the mirror, adjusting her jacket with a glazed expression. She appeared to be preparing for her date, yet her eyes seemed to see beyond the mirror. She was remembering one of her first dates out of college, several years before. At that time, Laurie was struggling with her identity in her entry level position and feeling that she should be doing much more with her fresh out of college education. What she had thought was confidence and charisma was perceived by others as the shaky bravado of an insecure young adult. A few years into her career and with a couple of relationships behind her, Laurie began to realize that being authentic and just being herself was all she was charged to be. It was so much easier than feigning intellect and pretending not to be afraid when she was actually terrified.

Laurie: Hi Mark – good to see you again.

Mark: Definitely my pleasure.

Laurie: There's a table over here if you don't mind sitting by the door.

Mark: No problem at all.

Laurie: I have to admit, I arrived an hour ago – completely forgot to double check the time!

Mark: No! You've been hanging around the entire hour?

Laurie: I have (*chuckling*.) But it worked out well as I caught my breath and did absolutely nothing for most of the hour. And I definitely saved myself from the worst of rush hour.

Mark: Well, I appreciate your waiting it out. Honestly, most people would've cancelled.

Laurie: Absolutely not. I really had a great time last week and really happy to see you again.

Mark: Well, me too. I thought I'd blown it when I told you my divorce just became final. My sister just texted me that I don't know a thing about what to say on a date!

Laurie: Hmmm... as you recall, I then told you that I had a young marriage that lasted less than a year.... I guess we're both writing our own rule books!

(*Laurie and Mark caught up on politics and shared more about their careers and lives outside work. Laurie wasn't aware that Mark's marriage had dissolved with conflict in the relationship predominately regarding finances and the false façade that his former spouse had projected to her friends. Mark had promised himself that he would not compare anyone to his past relationship, yet his vulnerabilities existed and he stumbled here and there. He feared that he was not very wise regarding women and had been told that he was easily taken advantage of in his relationships. He hoped to connect with someone who was honest and secure but doubted his own capacity to read people accurately.*)

Laurie: Mark? Is everything ok?

Mark: Oh! I'm sorry – I totally drifted off in my thoughts.

Laurie: Just let me know if you want to call it a night.

Mark: No, no, not at all. I was actually just reflecting on how comfortable you are. You really seem to know yourself.

Laurie: Thanks, Mark. (*Quips.*) Well, I guess you caught me on a good day! No, honestly -- I really do appreciate that. It means a lot.

(*Laurie and Mark finish their drinks and await the check. They compare calendars and plan when next they can meet.*)

Mark: Well, it's a school night so I guess we'd better not close the place down.

Laurie: True – I've got a presentation I need to polish tonight so I may run back to the office before heading home.

Mark: Ambitious!

Laurie: Ha! Nah, this is a pet project that I'm working on. I mean, don't get me wrong – there are some days that I'm totally pulling my hair out. But I love how my department is running right now.

Mark: That's a great work ethic. Your manager probably fears for his job.

Laurie: (*Laughing*) He was actually around when I was really green and painfully insecure. But he only had to tell me once that I needed to wake up. He said as soon as I took full responsibility for my own work, I'd be fine. I mean, he wasn't exactly scolding me, but he saw that I was sort of waiting around for someone to help me out when I really just needed to embrace the messiness of it all and clean it up myself.

Mark: Good manager.

Laurie: Definitely. And after a year or so, I started to catch on that as soon as I dug in and did my own navigating, good things would happen. I try to work with my direct reports with that same approach.

Mark: You're a task master!

Laurie: (*Chuckling*) Hardly! But my team definitely churns out a ton of work!

Mark: (*Sipping the last of his drink and nodding appreciatively*) Very attractive, you know.

Laurie: Ack! Well, I'm definitely not all work and no fun. And maybe sometimes work is just an acceptable excuse not to go out.

Mark: Well, I'm glad you came out tonight.

Laurie: Me too!

In recent years, Laurie had developed an internal source of strength and a more secure capacity to make relationship choices. She embraced her unique journey – a story of autonomy and fortitude. She found freedom in *choosing* a partner rather than in *needing* a partner. Desiring a partner is a very positive thing; needing a partner may be externalized as pressure and internalized as personal lacking.

It is long studied that humans have a fundamental need for affiliation -- we seem to be wired to be "with." Henry Murray was one of the first to develop a taxonomy of needs that included affiliation (Murray, 1938.) David McLelland and numerous other theorists have studied the importance of belongingness and affiliation within interpersonal relationships (McLelland, 1987.) Being a part of a community may be a critical component in your continued growth. Within the communities in your life, aim to contribute and participate in your own authentically genuine way. Pay attention to how you feel when you are self accepting. A predictor of your being accepted by others is your self acceptance and acceptance of others (Maslow, 1943.) This applies to a large community or a community of two. While the longing to belong may be fulfilled by larger systems, most humans thrive on the feelings of being prioritized.

Vulnerable Reflections on Relationships

Years ago, my fellow grad students, friends, and future colleagues were discussing what they wanted to find in a life partner. Many talked of having shared interests and the ability to laugh at the same things. Respect and trust were high ranking. Not surprisingly as psychology students, they emphasized the importance of empathy. But one person stood out in her vulnerable honesty, "I agree with you guys that I want someone who isn't threatened by my accomplishments and just says 'Yea!' if I do well. But I really want someone who cares about me no matter what. I'm not afraid to say that I want someone who will take care of me. (*The wise and seasoned study group gawked and laughed about the importance of autonomy.*) Hey guys, I can *totally* take care of myself. But I want someone who will not walk away when things are tough. And I don't want that person to hold that over me later on. I am willing to give that to a person. I really want to give that. All I want is that someone will give me what I'm ready to give. That seems fair. Doesn't it?"

Does it? This short book has examined some identifiers of healthy relationships and the discoveries you have made from your past relationships. While not exhaustive of all relationship literature, we have indeed found a prevailing theme of consistency in mutual respect, trust, fairness, empathy, and honesty. And while the teeter totter of a relationship is rarely a precise 50/50 split, there is a healthy and fair balance in a relationship where two people choose to give each other the same foundational bases of love.

We have noted that having the expectation of goodness yields a likelihood of mutual trust. Further, having individual happiness and satisfaction influences effective communication. And having respectful and empathic communication tends to fuel a tone of kindness and love. We have noted that these elements are "honest" and synchronized with a loving relationship. And if loving and respecting others begins with loving and respecting yourself, then starting with the person in the mirror seems a good place to commence your next steps toward healthy relationships.

Over time, you may find that you connect with someone who views you with mutual respect and trust. Aim to stay open and flexible as you listen, perspective take, and respond to each other. While your relationship history may be tapped, it will be helpful to apply the discoveries that you have made and allow yourself a clear view of the person without the intrusion of the negatives from your prior relationship. While it may be difficult to separate the past from the present, it is factual that the present person is not the former.

Final Thoughts

- Consistency in conveying love takes time – consistency cannot be rushed.
- Expecting a consistent conveyance of respect, trust, and fairness is normalcy.
- Emotional intimacy and physical intimacy evolve over time.

- To have honesty in the communication of love: Love must sound like love, look like love, and feel like love for a recipient to receive it as love.
- How people love and respect reflects how they self love and self respect.
- Being satisfied and happy helps people communicate.
- You have an infinite capacity to love and accept love. You can never use it all up.

And remember:

Champion your uniqueness.

Find your way to your unique happiness.

For you, there is not just one way – there are infinite paths to your unique happiness.

Your unique happiness increases the likelihood of finding your unique future.

References

Aronson, E., Akert, R.D., & Wilson, T.D. (2006). *Social psychology* (6th Ed.). Upper Saddle River, NJ: Pearson Prentice Hall.

Aronson, E., & Carlsmith, J.M. (1963). Effect of the severity of threat on the devaluation of forbidden behavior *Journal of Abnormal and Social Psychology, 66*(6), 584-588.

Beck, A, T.; Rush, A. J.; Shaw, B. F.; Emery, G. (1987). *Cognitive Therapy of Depression*. Guilford Press.

Benjamin, B, Weiss, G. (1946). *That Christmas Feeling.* RCA Victor, Artist Perry Como.

Bloomfield, L, Kendall, S, Applin, L, Dearnley, K, Edwards, L, Hinshelwood, L, Lloyd, P, Newcombe, T. (2004). *A qualitative study exploring the experiences and views of mothers, health visitors and family support centre workers on the challenges and difficulties of parenting.* Wiley Online Library. https://doi.org/10.1111/j.1365-2524.2005.00527

Bowlby, J. (1980). *Attachment and loss*: Vol. 3. Loss. New York, NY: Basic Books.

Campbell, J. (2002). *Health consequences of intimate partner violence*. Lancet. 2002;359:1331–1336.

Campbell, L., Simpson, J. A., Boldry, J. G., Rubin, H. (2010). *Trust, variability in relationship evaluations, and relationship processes*. Journal of Personality and Social Psychology, 99, 14.

Canfield, J.E. (2016). *Be your foundation: Be you. A psychologist's notes to clients.* New York: Image Cascade Publishing.

Canfield, J.E. (1994.) *Living in retirement and helping your parents enjoy retirement*. New York: Image Cascade Publishing.

Canfield, M.L. (2007). *Thriving Relationships*. New York: Image Cascade Publishing.

Canfield, M.L. (2002). *Performance as a function of feelings, thoughts, and contracts*. Image Cascade Publishing.

Clark, D.A., & Beck, A.T. (2010). *Cognitive therapy of anxiety disorders: Science and practice*. New York, NY: Guilford Press.

Clark, D.A., & Beck, A.T. (1999). *Scientific foundations of cognitive theory and therapy of depression*. New York, NY: Wiley.

Cooper, J. (2007). *Cognitive dissonance: Fifty years of a classic theory*, London: Sage publications.

Dewberry C., Juanchich M., & Narendran S. (2013). *Decision-making competence in everyday life: The roles of general cognitive styles, decision-making styles and personality*. Personality and Individual Differences, 55, 783–788.

Diener E. & Seligman M. E. P. (2002). *Very happy people*. Psychological Science, 13, 81–84.

Diener E., Emmons R. A., Larsen R. J., & Griffin S. (1985). *The satisfaction with life scale.* Journal of Personality Assessment, 49, 71–75.

Dymond, S, Dunsmoor, J, Vervliet, B, Roche, B, Hermans, D. (2015). *Fear Generalization in Humans: Systematic Review and Implications for Anxiety Disorder Research.* Behavior Therapy. 46 (5): 561–582.

Feeney, B, Van Vleet, M, Jakubiak, B, Tomlinson, J. (2017). *Predicting the pursuit and support of challenging life opportunities.* Personality and Social Psychology Bulletin, Volume: 43 issue: 8, page(s): 1171-1187

Festinger, L. (1985. [first published 1957]), *A theory of cognitive dissonance,* Stanford, CA: Stanford University Press Reissued by Stanford University Press 1962. Paperback.

Festinger, L., Riecken, H.W., & Schachter, S. (1956). *When prophecy fails.* Minneapolis: University of Minnesota Press.

Festinger, L., & Carlsmith, J.M. (1959). Cognitive consequences of forced compliance. *Journal of Abnormal and Social Psychology, 58*(2), 203-210.

Fiske, S. T., & Taylor, S. E. (1991). *Social cognition (2nd ed.)*. New York: McGraw-Hill.

Follingstad D, Coyne S, Gambone L. *A representative measure of psychological aggression and its severity.* Violence and Victims. 2005;20:25–38.

Gawronski, B., & Strack, F. (Eds.). (2012). *Cognitive consistency: A fundamental principle in social cognition.* New York: Guilford Press.

Geisler M, Allwood CM (2015). Competence and Quality in Real-Life Decision Making. PLoS ONE 10(11): e0142178. https://doi.org/10.1371/journal.pone.0142178

Goldstein, K. (1934). *The Organism: A Holistic Approach to Biology Derived from Pathological Data in Man.* New York: Zone Books, 1995

Goleman, D. (1995). *Emotional intelligence: Why it can matter more than IQ.* New York: Bantam Books.

Gravningen , K, Mitchell, K, Wellings, K, Johnson, A, Geary, R, Jones, K, Clifton, S, Erens, B, Lu, M, Chayachinda, C, Field, N, Sonnenberg, P, Mercer, C. (2017). *Reported reasons for breakdown of marriage and cohabitation in Britain: Findings from the third National Survey of Sexual Attitudes and Lifestyles(Natsal-3)* doi.org/10.1371/journal.pone.0174129

Halevy, N. *Preemptive strikes: Fear, hope, and defensive aggression.* Journal of Personality and Social Psychology, Vol 112(2), Feb 2017, 224-237

Harmon-Jones, E., & J. Mills. (Eds.) (1999). *Cognitive Dissonance: Progress on a Pivotal Theory in Social Psychology*. Washington, DC: American Psychological Association.

Hayes S.C, Wilson K.G., Gifford E.V, Follette V.M, Strosahl K. Experiential avoidance and behavioral disorders: A functional dimensional approach to diagnosis and treatment. Journal of Consulting and Clinical Psychology. 1996; 64:1152–1168.

Hazan, C, & Shaver, P. (1987). *Romantic love conceptualized as an attachment process.* Journal of Personality and Social Psychology. 52, 511-524.

Hazan, C, Shaver, P. (1994). *Attachment as an organizational framework for research on close relationships.* Psychological Inquiry. 5, 1-22.

Hegel, G.W.F. (1807/1977). *Hegel's Phenomenology of Spirit,* tr. A. V. Miller, 1977. [Translation from *Phanomenologie des Geistes,* 1807.]

Heidegger, M. (1962). *Being and Time.* Translated by John Macquarrie and Edward Robinson. London: SCM Press. [From original German: (1927). *Sein und Zeit.*]

Heider, F. (1958). *The Psychology of Interpersonal Relations*. New York: Wiley.

Jacobson NS, Margolin G. (1979). *Marital therapy: Strategies based on social learning and behavior exchange principles.* New York: Brunner/Mazel.

Kant, I. *Critique of Pure Reason* [1781], trans. Norman Kemp Smith (N.Y.: St. Martins, 1965)

Kelley, H. H. (1967). *Attribution theory in social psychology.* In D. Levine (ed.), Nebraska Symposium on Motivation (Volume 15, pp. 192-238). Lincoln: University of Nebraska Press.

Kim, H, Capaldi D, Crosby L. (2007). *Generalizability of Gottman and colleagues' affective process models of couples' relationship outcomes.* Journal of Marriage and Family. 69:55–72.

Knudson-Martin, C., Huenergardt, D., Lafontant, K., Bishop, L., Schaepper, J., & Wells, M. (2014). *Competencies for addressing gender and power in couple therapy: A socio-emotional approach.* Journal of Marital and Family Therapy, Advance online publication. doi: 10.1111/jmft.12068

Knudson-Martin, C. (2013). *Why Power Matters: Creating a Foundation of Mutual Support in Couple Relationships.* Family Process, Vol. 52, No. 1, 2013.

Knudson-Martin, C, Rankin-Mahoney, A. (2005). *Moving beyond gender: Processes that create relationship equality.* Journal of Marital and Family Therapy April 2005, Vol. 31, No. 2, 235–258

Lang, Peter J. (1994). *The Varieties of Emotional Experience: A Meditation on James–Lange Theory*. Psychological Review. 101 (2): 211–221.

Lavner, J, Karney, B, Bradbury, T. (2016). *Does couples' communication predict marital satisfaction, or does marital satisfaction predict communication?* Journal of Marriage and the Family. 2016 Jun 1; 78(3): 680-694.

Lewicki, R. J., McAllister, D. J., & Bies, R. J. (1998). *Trust and distrust: New relationships and realities*. Academy of Management Review. 23, 438-458.

Lewicki, R. J., & Wiethoff, C. (2000). *Trust, trust development, and trust repair.* In M. Deutsch & P. T. Coleman (Eds.), The handbook of conflict resolution: Theory and practice (pp. 86-107). San Francisco: Jossey-Bass.

Lewin, K. (1935). *A dynamic theory of personality: Selected papers.* New York: McGraw-Hill.

Luo S, Chen H, Yue G, Zhang G, Zhaoyang R, Xu D. (2008). *Predicting marital satisfaction from self, partner, and couple characteristics: Is it me, you, or us?* Journal of Personality. 76:1231–1266.

Markman, H, Rhoades, G, Stanley, S, Ragan, E, Whitton, S. (2010). *The premarital communication roots of marital distress and divorce: The first five years of marriage.* Journal of Family Psychology. 24:289–298.

Maslow, A. H. (1943). *A Theory of Human Motivation,* Psychological Review 50 :370-96

McClelland, D.C. (1987). *Human motivation.* New York: University of Cambridge.

McClelland, D.C., Atkinson, J.W., Clark, R.A., and Lowell, E.L. (1953). *The Achievement Motive.* NY: Appleton-Century-Crofts.

McClelland, D.C. (1951). *Personality.* NY: William Sloane Associates.

Murray, H. A. (1938). *Explorations in Personality*. New York: Oxford University Press

Pavlov, I.P. *Conditioned reflexes*. Oxford: University Press; 1927.

Random House Dictionary. New York: Random House, Inc., 2012.

Righetti, F, Visserman, M. (2017.) *I gave too much. Low self-esteem and the regret of sacrifices.* Social Psychological and Personality Science, Department of Social Psychology, Vrije Universiteit Amsterdam, Amsterdam, the Netherlands.

Sartre, Jean-Paul (2003). *Being and nothingness*. Hazel E. Barnes (trans.). London: Routledge.

Seligman M.E.P, Johnston J.C. *A cognitive theory of avoidance learning*. In: McGuigan F.J., Lumsden D.B, editors. Contemporary approaches to conditioning and learning. Washington, DC: Winston; 1973.

Shakespeare, W. (c. 1600). *Hamlet*.

Simpson, J, Drevets, W, Snyder, Z, Gusnard, D, Raichel, M. (2001). *Emotion-induced changes in human medial prefrontal cortex: II. During anticipatory anxiety.* Proc Natl Acad Sci U S A. 2001 Jan 16; 98(2): 688–693. doi: 10.1073/pnas.98.2.688

Skinner, B.F. (1938). *The behavior of organisms.* New York: Appleton-Century-Crofts.

Van der Kolk, B. (2014). *The body keeps the score: Brain, mind, and body in the healing of trauma.* New York: Penguin Books.

Visserman, M, Righetti, F, Kumashiro, M, Van Lange, P. (2017). *Me or us? Self-control promotes a healthy balance between personal and relationship concerns.* Social Psychological and Personality Science 8 (1), 55-65.

Woodin, EM. (2011). *A two-dimensional approach to relationship conflict: Meta-analytic findings.* Journal of Family Psychology. 25:325–335.

Film References

That Touch of Mink, (1962). Universal Pictures.

An Affair to Remember, (1957). Twentieth Century Fox Film Corporation.

The Heiress, (1949). Paramount Pictures, Corporation.

Now Voyager, (1942). Warner Brothers Films, Corporation.

Kitty Foyle, (1940). RKO Radio Pictures.

Respect. 2018. In *Merriam-Webster.com*. Retrieved April 4, 2018, from https://www.merriam-webster.com/dictionary/respect

Trust. 2018. In *Merriam-Webster.com*. Retrieved April 4, 2018, from https://www.merriam-webster.com/dictionary/trust

The Author

Dr. Joy Canfield is a licensed psychologist in New York City. With a unique background of solution focused, positive psychology, Dr. Canfield works with clients to create a healthful, balanced approach to optimistic living.